# PASSIVE IN

—————— ❧❦❧ ——————

*2 Manuscripts including blogging and dropshipping with Ideas and Strategies*

**Gary Loomer**

# Your Free Gift

As a way of saying thank you for your purchase, I wanted to offer you a free bonus e-book called **10 Easy Ways To Make $2k A Month Passively**

Download the free ebook here: https://www.subscribepage.com/business2k

What is passive income and how can it help you to quit your day job. Imagine going to sleep at night, and knowing that your bank accounts are filling up.

In this free guide, you'll discover what passive income and 10 lucrative strategies to earn $2k a month and more.

# Listen to this book for free

Do you want to be able to listen to this book whenever you want? Maybe whilst driving to work or running errands. It can be difficult nowadays to sit down and listen to a book. So I am really excited to let you know that this book is available in audio format. What's great is you can get this book for FREE as part of a 30-day audible trial. Thereafter if you don't want to stay an Audible member you can cancel, but keep the book.

Benefits of signing up to audible:

- After the trial, you get 1 free audiobook and 2 free audio originals each month
- Can roll over any unused credits
- Choose from over 425,000 + titles
- Listen anywhere with the Audible app and across multiple devices
- Keep your audiobooks forever, even if you cancel your membership

Click below to get started

Audible US - https://tinyurl.com/y5fcrzss

Audible UK - https://tinyurl.com/y2je946f

Audible FR - https://tinyurl.com/y5cndotr

Audible DE - https://tinyurl.com/y2lrs5c6

# TABLE OF CONTENTS

# BLOGGING

*For profit, passive income idea for making money working from home*

**Gary Loomer**

# TABLE OF CONTENTS

**BLOGGING**

# INTRODUCTION

Congratulations on downloading *Blogging: For profit, passive income idea for making money working from home* and thank you for doing so. The first step in becoming a popular blogger is to read this book for all of the great information within. The information in this book will help you get started with your blog. Don't hesitate to read this book. You will not be disappointed in the information within.

No matter what kind of content you want to create, the internet has a place for it. The internet gives you a chance to produce a blog, create products to sell, and how to monetize your blog. Making money off your blog is relatively simple and easy, though it does take hard work. With this book, you can quickly get a blog on the web and earn money from it.

The following chapters will discuss how to start, create, promote, and customize your blog along with information on how to make money off your blog and how to sell your own products. By selling products and services, you can take your blog to the next level. Within are also instructions on how to keep readers hooked and how to grow your audience. Within this **book**, you have all of the information to make a great blog.

There are plenty of books on this subject on the market, so thanks again for choosing this one!

Every effort was made to ensure it is full of as much useful information as possible. Please enjoy!

# CHAPTER 1: STARTING A BLOG

## What Is a Blog?

A blog is an online website where the blog's owner writes and produces content for an online readership or audience. Blogs are very commonly used online tools for getting the content to readers.

Before you can start blogging, you have to start a blog in the first place. How do you start a blog? The first thing you have to do is come up with a theme and a reason why you want to blog. Many people have different reasons for blogging. Some people want to blog just to tell the world about themselves while others use blogging as a tool for social change, and others even blog to sell products or to promote themselves. Each different type of blog is perfectly acceptable and a worthwhile goal. This chapter will explore the questions you should ask yourself before starting a blog.

The word blog started out as the early internet term Weblog. Those early web pages were pages of links to news and other websites, without much commentary. Over time, the word got compressed into "blog," and instead of pages full of links, the pages often became very personal, almost like an online diary. There are also very serious blogs found on the internet. Businesses often have blogs, as well as professional organizations. Really, anyone can start a blog and it can be about almost anything.

## Why Blog?

There are many reasons to blog. In order to start your blog, it helps if you know what those reasons are. Knowing your reasons for blogging helps you to know what kind of topics and content you want to have on your blog, and it can help you to narrow down your target audience. Do you want a professional sounding blog about politics, economics, or product reviews; or you could want a more laid-back site where you discuss your hobbies. Both the professional and laid-back blogs are appropriate for different audiences. Knowing which one you are writing for, however, can help you set the tone for your blog. If you are writing a very professional sounding blog, it should sound more formal. If you are writing a more laid-back blog, you probably want to make it sound less formal and more conversational. It all depends on what you want to accomplish with your blog.

## Before You Start

Before you start your blog, you should have a clear idea of what you want to accomplish with it and what kinds of content do you want to create. Do you want to sell products, do you want to comment on political issues, or do you want to support a game like Dungeons and Dragons or Fortnite? The reasons for having a blog are many and multifaceted, so having a clear idea of the kind of the content you want on your blog is essential to creating a lasting site.

It is also important to know what your overall message is before you start. Knowing your message allows you to present it to your readers in new and innovative ways. In order to find those innovative ways to express your message, you should research what is already out there on the subject or theme you want to blog about. Exposing yourself to the content that already exists lets you decide what works and what doesn't. This lets you refine your content for your target audience.

## Who Is Your Audience?

Once you know what you want to blog about and you know your message, the next thing to do is to figure out your target audience. Your target audience is who you want to read your blog. You should have a pretty clear idea of who you are writing for so that you can provide the kinds of content that people want to see. Knowing your audience goes a long way to making your blog successful.

To determine your target audience, ask yourself who is likely to read your content. In one of the examples above, a writer might want to write content for a Dungeons and Dragons blog. For a Dungeons and Dragons blog, you might want to write rules for the game, recount your characters' adventures, share personal drawings, or even stream online games to services like Twitch. Twitch is an online platform where you can stream video games online and other people can watch you play.

In order for you to build an effective Dungeons and Dragons blog, you first need to know who is going to read it. The typical Dungeons and Dragons player is an adult white male who plays games and is generally educated, as the game requires reading and knowledge of basic mathematics. These players fall into the category of geek or nerd, and it can be assumed that the person reading your blog also plays in other games. Knowing that they fall into the geek spectrum allows you to tailor your content for the reader. For instance, you might include content about other tabletop RPGs (role-playing games) such as the Star Wars or the Star Trek role-playing games. It also tells you that the reader most likely enjoys fantasy novels, which is another type of content that you can add. Knowing your target audience allows you to customize the content your readership wants.

An example of what is likely an unsuccessful blog would be one that has random cooking recipes, video game content, and mystery novels. While all three topics are interesting and can be explored, they don't have much in common, so it is difficult to find a readership that is interested in all three. If you do not have the focus around what type of content you create, it becomes difficult to keep your readers attention. Focusing on related topics lets you tailor your content to the people likely to read your blog.

# CHAPTER 2: CREATE A BLOG

Once you have the concept for your blog, the next step is to actually create the blog itself. This chapter explores getting a URL, the blogging tools you need, and several hosting options.

## Get a Domain Name

The first thing to do is to come up with your URL, also known as a domain name. A URL is an address that people use to load sites on the internet. For instance, Google's domain is www.google.com. When you want to go to Google, you just go to their domain. Blogs also have domain names, and the catchier they are, the better the chances that the reader will remember your site. The other difficulty with domain names is finding one that is not taken.

You can purchase a domain name from various places on the internet. Many internet hosting sites provide a domain name for a small fee, or in some cases, for free. Free domain names are rarely catchy or very unique, meaning that they are often difficult to remember, and that might drive traffic away from your blog. It is often easier to purchase a domain name directly from the hosting site that you choose to use. Purchasing your domain from the site you get hosting from makes sure that there are no issues with your domain pointing to your site correctly. When you purchase a domain from another site, there may be settings you need to adjust to make sure it works correctly.

## Blogging Tools

Each blog hosting website offers different blogging tools. There is no set industry standard so all of the hosting sites choose which features they want to include in their blogging tools. These tools range from plug-ins, widgets, templates, and other ways to customize your blog. Some sites offer more in terms of blogging tools than other hosting sites, but the tools offered have to be weighed against the cost of the hosting services. There is more on what tools are available for the various hosting services later in this chapter.

An obstacle that is often overwhelming is coding. Coding is an immense challenge. Coding means that you write the computer code that tells your reader's web browser how the webpage should look. An example of how coding can improve your site is by allowing you to bold certain text for emphasis. Another example is coding a pop-up window to show up on your site, perhaps to offer an email subscription service.

The internet runs on a programming language called hypertext markup language or HTML. This language allows bloggers to make changes to her or his website via the actual code of the site. However, a large number of bloggers do not code but use the built-in blogging tools to mimic HTML without having to write the code themselves. This is why hosting sites make blogging tools so useful.

They allow you to create the content you want without having to write computer code.

An example of how blogging tools deviate from coding HTML is the example of bold text. To bold text in HTML, you need to use HTML tags to do it. HTML tags are designed to change the text by having an opening set of angular brackets <> with the HTML command inside. Next, you have the text or content that the HTML tag is modifying, and finally, the closing set of brackets with a forward slash </> that indicates the HTML tag should stop.

Tags appear in the following form:

The word(s) you want to appear as <bold>This Text</bold> text.

This will appear on the screen as:

The word(s) you want to appear as **This Text**.

Many blogging tools, on the other hand, lets you simply highlight the text you want to bold and then you press a button to change it to bold.

While blogging tools make it easier to do simple things like controlling bold text, they often have difficulty with complex sites. Hence, coding has not gone out of the window altogether. Also, using blogging tools instead of coding means that you ultimately give up some control over how your page looks and acts.

## Ways to Customize Your Blog

There are three main ways to customize your blog. They are widgets, plug-ins, and themes. These three customization options allow you to carefully craft your own blog. Below are descriptions of the three:

**Widget:** A widget is an app that can be added to your blog when using certain hosting sites such as Blogger. Widgets are generally free and are often made by coders on the internet. You can locate a large number of widgets available for download from the internet. Widgets are basically add-ons for your blog that add additional functionality to your site.

**Plug-Ins:** Plug-ins are like widgets, but are used on different blogging platforms. For instance, you will find plug-ins used in the WordPress software, whereas, widgets are used in Blogger.

**Themes:** Themes are pre-built pages that you can start with. They include the graphic layout or where things go on the webpage of the blog. Themes can change things like the font style or where the navigation buttons appear on the webpage. Blogging and website themes are very common. Many users make their own and then share them for free or at little cost. Keep in mind, however, that many themes are not made with blogs in mind. When you are looking at themes, however, keep in mind that not all of them are made for blogging sites and may be aimed at different types of websites such as a business or government website.

Each of these customization options and more will be covered in detail in Chapter 6.

# WordPress.org

WordPress.org is a website that hosts the WordPress software. The WordPress software is the best software package for blogging and possibly for making a website. It has the most options, widgets, plug-ins, and customization options available for any blogging software. WordPress has an extensive library of plug-ins and themes, giving you many options to choose from. To help you stay focused on blogging themes, just search for the blog in the WordPress search to find appropriate themes for your site. You can download many options from the WordPress site that you can add or download for your blog. Some blogging platforms allow you to import WordPress options.

WordPress.org should not be confused with WordPress.com. WordPress.org provides the blogging software that is also called WordPress while WordPress.com is a hosting site where the blog is stored on a server. You can upload the files you download from WordPress.org to your WordPress.com site.

## Hosting Options

There is a wide range of hosting options for several blogging platforms. Hosting sites often work on a tiered system of packages. They will offer between roughly 3 to 5 packages that you can choose from with the more expensive packages having more options than the free or cheaper packages. Hence, the more you pay the more things you can do with your blog. Also, more expensive packages come with better features such as monetizing your blog with an online store or with paid advertisements. The more expensive packages also allow you to remove ads that the hosting site puts on your page. This means that any ad revenue that is generated goes to you and not the hosting company.

Below is a list of hosting website, their pros and cons, and their pricing structure.

## Blogger

Blogger is Google's blogging platform. Blogger is a good option if you want an easy-to-use service that does not require any coding.

**Pros:** The biggest pro for Blogger is that it is free. Blogger is also very easy to use and does not require coding knowledge.

**Cons:** Blogger has very basic blogging tools which makes it difficult to customize your blog. Blogger also has a very limited number of templates available. The third-party templates available for Blogger tend to be poorly made.

## Price: Free

## Wix

Wix is a website that offers internet hosting and is great for blogging. Wix features a very robust website that is very stable and has many options for customization.

**Pros**: Setup for Wix is very easy. Wix features dozens of templates, widgets, and apps. Wix is also good because the site is made by dragging and dropping elements, thus, no coding knowledge is needed. Another pro is that you can add other types of pages to a Wix blog like a forum.

**Cons:** The cons for Wix include a poor selection of third-party apps, once you choose a template, it cannot be changed. The eCommerce options are restricted to paid plans. The free plan for Wix is very limited.

**Price:** Free, but there are paid plans available. To purchase a domain name, it is $4.50 per month. The premium plans range from $8.50 to $24.50 per month.

## Weebly

Weebly is another blogging platform. It is easy to use and requires no technical or coding skills.

**Pros**: Weebly has a free plan that lets you try out their features. It also boasts a simple to use setup, and the blogging tools are very easy to use.

**Cons:** Weebly's main problem is that the blogging tool features are limited and you cannot add additional features. Weebly also has problems with exporting your site to another platform and it has poor integration with third-party add-ons.

**Price:** Weebly is free but there are monthly plans ranging from $8.00 to $49.00 per month.

# Tumblr

Tumblr is a different type of blogging platform. This is because Tumblr is built as both a microblogging platform as well as being closely integrated with social media. Microblogging is where you make short blog posts such as just an image or gif. Microblogging typically requires you to make very frequent microblog posts.

**Pros**: Tumblr is very easy to use with social media built into the platform. Tumblr also makes it very easy to share videos and other content quickly.

**Cons:** Tumblr has a very limited number of features. Also backing up or moving your blog to another platform is very difficult.

**Price:** Tumblr is free. You can add a custom domain name for an additional charge.

# Squarespace

Squarespace is another website hosting site where you can have your blog. Squarespace does not offer free memberships. All of their services require a premium membership. Squarespace is designed primarily for small businesses so it offers domain names with SSL/HTTPs and an eCommerce store.

**Pros**: Strong support for an eCommerce website. Squarespace is easy to use and does not require coding skills. Squarespace also features very professional templates.

**Cons:** There are a limited number of features and because Squarespace uses a unique platform, there are no third-party apps, widgets, or plug-ins. This really limits the ability to customize your blog. The Personal plan also only gets you your blog, 20 pages, and two contributors.

**Price:** Pricing for Squarespace's Personal membership is $16 per month if billed monthly or $12 a month if you purchase your membership annually. The Business plan starts at $26 a month or $18 per month if it is billed annually.

## WordPress.com

As mentioned above, Wordpress.com is a site that hosts blogs and other websites. WordPress is a good blend of easy to use with all the power of the WordPress software behind it.

**Pros**: WordPress is built specifically to use WordPress software, which means, it is easy to build a blog, and there is extensive third-party support for apps, plug-ins, and templates.

**Cons:** You cannot put your own ads on a WordPress blog. This limits your ability to monetize your site.

**Price:** WordPress offers a free plan but it comes with the WordPress logo and ads. Upgrading to a Personal Plan removes the logo and ads. You can also get a custom domain. The upgrade costs $2.99 a month. Another upgrade for $8.25 a month, billed annually, gets extra storage and design options.

# Ghost

Ghost is another web hosting site for your blog. It differs from other blogging platforms because it is for the technically minded user. It is easy to use if you are a coder. Allowing you to use coding strongly on the site gives you a level of control over the page that is missing on other blogging platforms. Other sites rely heavily on templates that you cannot alter very much, but Ghost allows you to alter the actual code of the page, making it one of the best blogging platforms for customization.

**Pros:** As stated above, Ghost gives you a lot of control over how the page looks and acts. Ghost is also open source, which means that software is easily available to third-party software designers. Ghost also shows you a live view of what your page will look like.

**Cons:** You really need to have the technical knowledge to use Ghost. If you are just starting out and do not know HTML, then Ghost most likely is not a good option for you.

**Price:** Ghost offers a free 14-day trial. After that, Ghost has a Basic package starting at $36 a month or $29 if billed annually and range to $249 or $199 a month if billed annually.

# CHAPTER 3: KEEP READERS HOOKED

Once you have your blog started, chosen a domain name, and set up an account with the blogging platform of your choice, the next thing to do is start creating content for your blog. The following chapter will discuss how to create content that keeps your readers coming back for more. This chapter will cover the basics of how to create content and how to respond to current trends.

## Generating Content

Generating content is the cornerstone of any blog. If you do not have regular content, it makes it difficult for people to know when to check your site. This can be alleviated somewhat by having an email list, but regular updates are a better bet. Rarely updated blogs do not get much attention.

There are several types of content that you can create. The most basic type of content is writing the blog posts. All blogs need words and writing is often the best way to make your point or to discuss a subject. Not only should blog posts be frequent, but they should also be at least 1,000 words long. 1,000 words might sound daunting, but it is a good length to keep readers interested in what you have to say. Shorter blog posts, unless updated very frequently such as in microblogging, might not be interesting to your readers. It is difficult to make a good point in less than 1,000 words. By the same logic, however, too many words are often a turn-off for the casual reader. Instead, you need to find a good middle place where you have blog posts that are detailed, but that is not too long.

However, blogs don't have to just be words on the page. They can also include photos, infographics, charts, and videos. In fact, video blogs are their own medium and are referred to as vlogs. Vlogs are popular on YouTube and on streaming services like Twitch. Vlogs are typically updated every day, or sometimes, multiple times a day.

Once you decide what medium you want to use for your content, the next step is to create that content. Of course, you will add to the blog each time you post to it, but it is a good idea to have quite a bit of content ready to go so that when you first start your blog, you already have posts ready to go.

## Responding to Trends

A great way to keep readers hooked is to respond to the various fads and trends on the internet. By engaging with these trends, you can create content that is fresh and is currently popular. An example of this is a cooking blog where you post recipes. Instead of posting just any recipe, you notice that there is a fad where people are posting vegan recipes on social media. To adapt to the trend, you start including more vegan recipes on your blog. Including the trend in your blog makes you sure it is up-to-date as well as providing the recipes that your readership wants. In the above case, you can also provide nutrition information for your recipes. Staying on top of new diets and fads can help your recipe blog.

In order to properly respond to trends and fads, you must first be aware of what those trends are. An easy way to do this is to keep on top of social media apps like Twitter and Facebook. Twitter has a listing of trending topics that you can follow, but a more effective way to stay on top of trends is to identify several people who are involved in delivering the content that you want. By finding those people and watching their blog or social media accounts, you can keep an eye on what they are posting. This will show you the trends that you need to follow in order to keep up with trends.

Another way to follow trends is to follow hashtags. Hashtags are tags on Twitter and Facebook that help people to follow a certain topic. By following hashtags, you can stay up-to-date about trends. In fact, when hashtags go viral, they are referred to as "trending". Hashtags appear with a hash symbol "#" at the beginning and then a phrase afterward. An example is #startrekfans, which is a hashtag for Star Trek fans. Hashtags are often current news, something a celebrity says, or really anything.

## Being Helpful

One of the most important things you can do with your blog is to be helpful to your readers. Being helpful means that the reader (or viewer if it is a vlog) finds whatever content you create as useful for their lives. An example of this is a self-help blog where the blogger gives good information about how to enhance your life or improve your health. By giving helpful information, you keep your readers' attention and they keep coming back for more.

Another thing you can do to be helpful is to be engaged with your readers. You can do this by responding to comments left on your blog posts. By becoming actively involved with your readers, you can increase your connection with them. Sometimes, this level of personal attention takes too long and you may not be able to engage with very many readers.

## Be Unique

Another way to keep your readers hooked is to be unique. Being unique lets your readers always get something new from your blog posts. This fresh content will keep your readers coming back for more. To be unique, you just have to have a new and different take than the other blogs and website on your subject(s). Following trends and other people in your subject area helps you to know what is overused or talked about too much. When you are exposed to this other content, you can choose to take a different path.

One way to be unique is to research your subject thoroughly before you begin to write. By educating yourself on the topic and researching it, you can get in-depth information that other blogs or website might not have. For instance, you might quote a study or an expert (see below for more information on experts).

Another way to be unique is to share information from personal experiences. Drawing from your life allows you to have a fresh and personal take on the issue or subject, whereas, someone who is not sharing personal details will generally not come across as genuine and will lose readership. An example of how to share personal information is by telling stories.

## Tell Stories

Humans have been telling stories throughout our civilization. Telling stories has bound people together, and storytelling has evolved from the humble beginning in early humans to the expressive books and movies of today. Using stories in your blog posts can let you harness that narrative power for yourself.

Telling stories helps you not only to be unique and genuine, but it is a compelling way to engage with your audience. Telling stories in your blog posts allows you to connect directly with your readership. By adding stories, you can engage with your readers in new and different ways. Not only will your blog seem more genuine, using stories in your blog lets you describe things in a narrative style. People tend to respond well to blog posts that use the narrative format. Giving information in a story also lets you make your point without being overly didactic, even if you are giving specific advice to your readers.

Telling stories also helps people to see your point without it becoming dry or repetitive. Using stories helps keep the blog posts interesting, fresh, and new. Stories also help to keep your reader's attention on the subject you are writing about.

Another way to use storytelling in your blog posts is to illustrate examples by using narrative storytelling. By illuminating examples with stories, you can give detailed information without it being dry and stale. With stories, you can make those examples come to life just by telling them in a story format. Your readers will enjoy stories on your blog.

## Quote Experts

One way to hook your readership is to quote facts and experts. By quoting experts, you strengthen any rhetorical arguments or informative content you have. Quoting experts helps you to sound professional. Including facts and quotes makes you sound reliable, which increases your readership's trust and helps to solidify your reader's respect for you.

Quoting experts and facts is also a great way to meet those 1,000 words that each blog post should be. While quoting experts might take some research, it means that there are fewer words you need to write in order to make the 1,000-word count. Quoting experts might also lead to you using infographics or charts, which also make your blog appear trustworthy and professional.

# Use Images and Videos

Another way to keep your readers interested is by using images, charts, and videos. Using images and videos works to keep your readers attention on your page, and it helps to keep your blog graphically interesting, which goes a long way to keep your readers reading your blog. Using graphics is also a way to incorporate facts into your page which, as discussed above, makes your blog look much more professional.

**Photos:** Photos are the most basic graphic that you can put on your blog. Pictures can be of anything that helps your blog be informative or helpful to the reader. Photos can be of products that you are reviewing, items that you are using, prepared food, and even pictures of yourself. The point of adding photos is to make the blog more visual and to introduce a way to convey your point using photos, even if they are just meant as humor or other types of entertainment.

**Videos:** Videos go a long way to making your blog successful, and most of the time, they are pretty simple to make. You don't have to have a vlog or microblogging in order to have videos. Most smartphones can make videos that have quality high enough to share on your blog. Videos let you connect to your readers or viewers. Videos also work as an easy way to communicate with your readers. Conveying information via video instead of your readers always having to read your page, gives them a chance to sit back and receive the information via video. Regular videos set the reader's expectations that you will have a steady amount of video content.

**Infographics:** Infographics are graphics that are meant to share specific information. An example of an infographic is a map of the United States with the blue states representing that the state is a Democrat-controlled state and the red states stand for the Republican Party. This simple graphic has a large amount of information available at a glance. You don't have to use infographics only in the more professional or formal blogs, you can use also use them in more hobby oriented blogs.

**Charts:** Another kind of image you can use on your blog is a chart. You might want charts to illustrate a concept that you are discussing. Like infographics, charts can relay a lot of information in simple graphics. Charts differ from infographics because of the format. Charts tend to be pie charts, Venn diagrams, or line charts. An example of a blog that might use charts is a health-related or nutrition blog. These blogs might have information that is typically displayed as charts, so you want to mimic the other sites and blogs that use the information. These graphics help you to have a professional looking blog, as well as conveying the information effectively.

## Guest Bloggers

Another way to keep your readers interested is to have guest bloggers. Guest bloggers bring their own unique content and can offer a fresh take on the subjects or issues your blog discusses. Some guest bloggers expect payment, but the majority of bloggers will see it as a chance to gain exposure to your readership and will be happy to guest blog for free. You can use a guest blogger for a single blog post, or you can ask them to curate your blog for a few days or more. For instance, a poetry blog might have a guest blogger be in charge of editing the poetry on the site for a few days as opposed to the poetry you receive through your regular submission process.

Guest blogging also works very well because it allows you a chance to take a break or concentrate on getting longer works of your own content ready while the guest blogger keeps your readers interested.

## Hire Help

Lastly, you can always hire a freelance writer to write blog posts for you. There are several websites out there that offer articles to be written for you. An example of this kind of website is www.textbroker.com. Textbroker has a staff of writers and editors who write content on an as-needed basis. You don't get one dedicated writer, but your blog posts might come from any of the writers they have on staff.

If you're enjoying this book, I would appreciate it if you went to the place of purchase and left a short positive review. Thank you.

# CHAPTER 4: PROMOTE YOUR BLOG IN CREATIVE WAYS

There are many ways to promote your blog from using social media to search engine optimization. This chapter will take a look at some creative and effective ways to promote your blog, which in turn, increases your readership. By using some creative and tried-and-true ways, you can grow your readership by promoting your blog.

## Headlines

When you are writing your blog posts, the headlines you choose are very important. The headline is the first thing that someone will read about your blog post. When you share links on social media, the headline is typically displayed with a link to the article, so with that headline, you have a chance to grab the readers' attention and bring them to your blog.

Writing effective headlines can be difficult, but it is necessary to write them. Good headlines are both informative and catchy. Being informative is very important as it gives the reader a reason to read the article. However, you can take this to the extreme and only have an informative headline, whereas, a catchy headline helps increase the readers desire to find out what the blog post has to say.

It should also be noted that your headlines should not be misleading. Misleading headlines often causes posts to be considered spam, fake news, or in a specifically bad situation, it might be called trolling. This lowers the trust your readers have in your blog and can cause you to seem unprofessional. An example of a fake news headline is "cannabis cures cancer". While there is some research that suggests this is true, the statement is not scientifically proven, so the headline is misleading. Meanwhile, if you were to say: "studies show promise that cannabis cures cancer", the headline is factual, provides information, and draws the reader in, all without resorting to hyperbole or becoming misleading.

## Share Your Posts

Another creative way to promote your blog is to share your posts. You can share your posts either using social media (see below) or you can share your blog posts on forums or on the comments pages of a website, especially if it is a specific website for your subject. Using forums is very effective as you can interact directly with people on a forum and you can direct them to your blog by sharing an interesting post or two. An example of this is if you have a health blog and you go to a website about diabetes and shared a blog post you wrote on the subject with the community there. If the community likes the article, one or several of the people on that site might begin frequenting your blog.

## Email Lists

While they are not as prevalent as they used to be, email lists can still be a useful way to connect to your readers. You can set up an email list so that every time you make a blog post or have an announcement, an email is sent to everyone that has signed up for your list. You might also want to use an email list to deliver upcoming information about your blog. If you have a video on your blog post, you can include a link to the video on YouTube (see social media below).

A very effective use of an email is a newsletter that collects all of your blog and social media posts that go out weekly or every few days. This gives your readers a chance to get all the posts at once.

Studies show that you should send out the same content out by email multiple times. The second or third time you send the email, you can customize it with a new summary or perhaps a different photo or graphic.

A percentage of your readership might miss the first email or not open it. Sending the content out multiple times gives the reader multiple chances to open the email. This greatly increases your chance that the email will be opened by the reader.

You might use an email list if your blog is used to promote your music career and you want your fans and readers to know about your upcoming gigs or concerts. Another example of a useful email list is an author using it to notify the readers that a new book is out and where they can make purchases of it.

**Social Media**

Social media has already been discussed. However, it is one of the best ways to promote your blog posts. Social media makes it easy to post about your blog on your wall, in groups, and in comments. You can use hashtags to start your own trends and get retweeted by other people, spreading your blog post throughout the internet. If you are lucky, you might even go viral, which is sure to bring in a large new crowd for your blog. Since social media accounts are such a good way to get information about your blog out, you should always have a link to your blog in your various social media accounts.

Below are several social media platforms and how you can use them to promote your blog.

**Twitter**

The first social media platform is Twitter. Twitter has millions of users from all over the globe. You can connect with Twitter by just making an account. The first thing that you should do with a Twitter account is to fill out all the profile information and make it clear that you have a blog. Making a post on Twitter is referred to as a tweet.

The next thing you should do is to find or follow some hashtags that are related to your blog so that you can find out what is out there on your subject.

Once you have done that, you should be able to identify several people with shared interests that you can connect to and become friends. Becoming friends on Twitter is the key to getting the word out about your blog. Once you become friends with people and begin interacting with them, you should start seeing more friend requests from shared friends.

Because Twitter has a restriction of 280 characters in their posts, it is easy to make short posts that are quick and punchy. Marketing experts recommend that you tweet at least 15 times a day. You can include links to your blog in the Tweet so that each post points back to your blog.

You can also interact with people on Twitter by using Direct Messaging (DM), where you can message someone directly without it being a public post that anyone can see. Using DM, you can begin directly interacting with the other people interested in what your blog is about. Once you have a relationship with someone you DM, it becomes more likely that they will retweet your tweets and blog posts.

**Facebook**

Another social media platform that you can use to promote your blog is Facebook. Facebook works a little differently than Twitter, with users having an unlimited number of characters. A lot of the same techniques you used with Twitter also work with Facebook. You can make friends, have a detailed profile, and send private messages (Facebook's version of DMing). How Facebook differs from Twitter is that hashtags are not as prevalent, and it has groups that you can comment in or self-promote in.

Some Facebook groups do not allow advertising or self-promotion, but many do. Some groups even have dedicated threads for self-promotion where you can have your blog alongside other blogs and ads. Another good thing about Facebook is that you can comment in many groups. So, for instance, if you have a health blog, you might post about your blog in general health, diabetes, weight loss, and nutrition groups. In this case, the vastness of Facebook can work to your advantage.

Another thing you can do on Facebook is to promote your posts. Promoting your posts costs money, but it exposes your Facebook posts to a much wider audience than you generally have, as many of your posts on your wall will only be seen by people who know you or are friends of your friends. Of course, this does not apply to groups where your posts are exposed to a lot of people, just your own wall.

You can also purchase ads on Facebook. Purchasing ads are more expensive than promoting posts, but by purchasing ads, you can target your audience. An example is the Dungeons and Dragons blog. Because you know that the majority of your audience is white males, aged 18-45, you can choose that demographic for your ad and it will appear in your target audience's feeds.

This type of advertising relies on you knowing your target audience which allows you to tailor ads for potential readers.

## YouTube

Finally, you have YouTube. YouTube is not a text-based social media platform, instead, it is a site filled with videos of every kind including vlogs, music videos, old TV shows, movies, and more. There is essentially any kind of video you want to watch.

Videos are collected into "channels," which are feeds with videos from the same poster. If you are making videos for your blog, even if it is not primarily a vlog, you can post those videos to YouTube for free. If you use videos, YouTube is an essential tool.

Not only can you host videos of yours, but if you get enough people like your videos or subscribe to your channel, you can also improve your reputation and get more views. When you get enough subscribers to your channel, you get into better positions on the site where more people can see your videos. If you gain enough subscribers, you can even get a premium account where you can have ads on your channel that earn you ad revenue.

## Google Ads

Another good way to promote your blog is to purchase a Google ad. Google ads are very effective because they can get displayed across a variety of mediums such as on smartphones or in the Google search results. Google ads are very useful in monetizing your blog.

**Clean Up Graph Data**

When you share your blog posts on social media, information about the blog post is used to create a shortcut. This typically displays a graphic of your page and a brief summary or the first part of your blog post. This is referred to as graph data. While the graph data is generally created automatically, you can access the data. This allows you to write a better introduction to your blog posts, any icons, and the artwork used in the graph data. You can access the graph data with a few different WordPress (the software, not the hosting site) plug-ins.

**Contests**

Another way to get and keep readers is to hold a contest. Because people enjoy having the chance to win something, you can draw them in with a contest. The prize can be anything from a book or a product you created yourself for sale in your eCommerce store.

You can easily spread a contest throughout the internet using your social media accounts. Many online contests like this require the participant to share a link to the contest on their own social media accounts. This expands the chance for other people to see the contest post, which leads to them checking out the rest of your blog.

# Chapter 5: Grow Your Audience

Every blog needs to expand and grow their audience, and your blog will be no exception. As you start posting on a regular basis, your blog should continue to gather new readers or viewers. This chapter will discuss various methods that you can use to increase the size of your audience.

## Search Engine Optimization

One very important aspect of growing your audience is the search engine optimization (SEO). SEO is the system by which a search engine catalogs your page for the engine's search results. Search engines scour pages for keywords that allow the search engine to properly rank your page. Search engines look for the keywords throughout the document to see how closely your blog is tied to your subject matter, whatever that might be. Keywords can be found in the header of the webpage and in the text of that page.

## Header Text

The first place that a search engine looks for keywords is in the header of the page. The header of the page is a part of a webpage that holds information about what the page is about. It does this by listing keywords. Many websites get poor results even though the webpage is well constructed, but because the page was not SEO, the search engine ranked it lower on the search results.

In the header of your page, you need to list every word you can find that is related to what your site is about. The search engine will see how many times those words appear in the header and the text of the page.

Below is an example header text for a work-out blog:

health, work out, gym, gyms, gymnastics, stretch, stretches, weight-lifting, ab, abs, crunch, crunches, leg lifts, treadmill, cardio, yoga, nutrition, carb, carbs, carbohydrate, carbohydrates, run, running, ran, CrossFit, boot camp, weight loss, fiber, heart, heart healthy

Notice how the header text uses several related words, even with such a subtle difference by using a plural versus a singular word. By building up large lists of keywords, you can make sure that the search engine ranks you highly on the search results.

## Repeating Keywords or Phrases

Another way to have SEO on your blog is to repeat key phrases and keywords throughout the text of your blog. The more times that you have an instance of a word in your text, the higher the search engine ranks your site. To get the most out of a blog post, you should repeat your main phrase and keywords several times throughout the text. For instance, you may use the word "health" seven times in a blog post about being healthy and eating right. If you have a business name that is associated with your blog, you should also repeat it several times. SEO techniques help you to make sure that the search engine ranks you appropriately.

## SEO Tools

Some blogging platforms offer SEO tools, sometimes at an additional cost, so that you can use the tools to develop an effective SEO strategy. Tools like these can be very useful when building your website in order to get those keywords into the header text of the page and throughout your website.

## Marketing Websites

Sometimes, it can be difficult to know what keywords to use in your header text or the phrases you need to repeat in order to get good SEO results. That is where BuzzSumo and Semrush come in handy. BuzzSumo and Semrush are websites used for marketing purposes. With these sites, you can search a website or keyword and get information about marketing the word.

An excellent way to use BuzzSumo and Semrush is to find a leading blog or website along with the same lines as your blog and to put that blog into the marketing website's search. The marketing website will then give you a list of content that is associated with the keyword or the website.

The website also offers an analysis of how the keyword or phrase responds. You can see information like the number of articles that are analyzed, the total number of shares, and the average number of shares. It also includes some useful charts that help you to understand the information easily. However, the additional analysis can cost extra. BuzzSumo offers a 14-day free trial. Semrush is somewhat more expensive with plans starting at $99.95 per month to $399.95 a month. The cost can be outweighed by the information you receive though.

The other thing that the marketing website can do is to help you to narrow down your target audience. With the marketing information available to you, the analysis can help you to figure out exactly who reads the content similar to your blog. This helps you to identify readers who are likely to read your blog.

## Forum Posts

Another way to grow your audience is to go on forum website and comment in them. You should be able to identify forums along the same lines as your blog. By becoming active in the forum, you can meet other people interested in the subject of your blog. When meeting these people, you can refer them to your blog. This allows you to engage with potential readers. You can begin following them in social media and by engaging with them, you increase the likelihood that they will become readers.

Forums generally allow you to have graphics and text at the bottom of your forum posts. This text and graphics are called a banner. You can use this banner to your advantage and put a blurb and an image of your blog as the banner signature. This means that every forum post you make automatically has a link back to your blog. This helps to direct the possible reader to your blog as possible, which can also lead them to an eCommerce store.

## Comments

Just like forum posts, leaving comments on other blogs and web pages is a way to engage the public and to grow your readership. When you comment on certain posts, you can always give a brief comment or explanation and then refer the readers back to your blog where you can have a more lengthy discussion of the topic. You can refer readers back to your blog by having a link to your blog in the comment you leave on the other website.

You can find many web pages to comment on. You can comment on other blogs that are similar or related to your own. Leaving comments on such a website can expose that blog or website's readers to you and your own content. By having engaging content, you can draw the reader or viewer in. Once the reader is hooked, they can become a part of your readership.

Types of websites that you can comment on include:

- Similar website
- Similar blogs
- Related YouTube videos

## Network with Other Bloggers

Something else you can do to increase your audience is to network with other bloggers. You can seek out other bloggers who might be helpful in locating new readers for your blog. By connecting with other bloggers, you can cross-promote each other's blog. This comes in handy even if the other person's blog is not similar or related to your own. Even though it might not be aimed at your specific target audience, it is still a chance to get exposure to more potential readers.

You can network with other bloggers by commenting on their blog posts or by finding them on social media and becoming friends. After you become friends, you can begin talking in your posts or through direct or private messaging. Once you have successfully networked with the other bloggers, you can begin to have them post links to your blog while you can do the same for them. That way both of you are potentially gaining new readers and/or social media followers.

## Following You

The next thing you can do to grow your audience is to encourage your readers to follow you on social media. When your regular readers add you to their social media accounts, their friends and followers will have a chance to see your content, and that can lead to new readers. Also, by having your readers follow you, you can give them extra opportunities to see your content.

Having your readers follow you allows you to engage with them in a way that you cannot with your blog alone.

## Engage With Your Readers

Next, you need to engage with your readers. You can do this by having the comments turned on for your posts. As people respond to your blog or video posts, you can respond and engage with your readers. You should be friendly and show respect to your readers, even if they disagree with you in the comments section. Disagreement can lead to some in-depth conversations that allow you to become closer to your readership.

Some ways that you can engage with your readership are:

> • Be accessible to your readers. If you are unreachable to your audience, they will have a more difficult time engaging with your blog. You should be very open to communicating with your readership. To make yourself available, you can add a contact page. A contact page is a page with information on how to reach you.

> • Avoid using "no reply" email addresses for your communications with your readers. It helps readers if they are

able to hit respond and contact you as opposed to having to locate another link or email address to respond to you. By not using a "no reply" email address, you can stay in close communication with your readership.

• You should attempt to respond to your readers. Regardless of if they send you an email, a direct message, or a private message, you should reply to your reader. Responding allows you to have a strong connection with the reader and should cement them as a regular to your blog.

• Finally, you can involve your readers in your blog and the content you create. You can do this by encouraging them to interact with the blog. A good example of this kind of contact with your readers is a simple poll. By having the poll on your site, you can determine what kind of content your readers want to see next, or you can evaluate how your previous content has worked out. You can often find this information out simply by asking your readers.

## Contribute On Other Blogs

Just as it's useful to have a guest blogger on your site, it is equally useful for you to guest blog on another site. By guest blogging, you have the ability to wow and bring in new readers to your blog. You should write a compelling blog post when you guest blog. If you put your best work forward, it doesn't just help you cement your relationship with the other blogger, but it also exposes your blog and writing to another audience. That exposure can lead to a larger number of readers for your own blog. You should strive to be a guest blogger on the best website out there. Being a guest blogger for major sites may lead to a large amount of exposure for you.

Before you approach another blogger, you should first network with them by leaving comments on their blog, emailing them, friending them on social media, tweeting, or sending direct or personal messages with the other blogger. Once you have a relationship with them, you should take the next step and pitch an idea for a post to them.

When you engage in guest blogging, you should make sure to link that blog out in your email list and posts on your social media accounts. This lets your regular readers know that there is a post on another blog for them to read.

# CHAPTER 6: CUSTOMIZE YOUR BLOG

Customizing your blog is important so that your page stands out and is unique. However, before you can customize your blog, you first need to be familiar with the various parts of a blog page. This chapter will cover the elements of a blog and the fundamentals of customization. It will also cover the WordPress software and the options you have with the software to customize your page.

## Elements of a Blog

Every blog has certain elements that are the same no matter what blogging platform or software you are using. These elementals are all customizable, allowing you to alter them to fit your needs. By changing these elements, you can control how your blog looks and acts. Changing these settings also allow you to make your blog original and unique. Below are the elements of the blog page and how you can customize them.

## Logo

The first and one of the most important aspects of the page is the logo on your page. You can have a picture of yourself or a logo from logo creation software, but using a professionally made logo goes a long way to having a unique blog. Your page is often judged by how professional it looks, even if the content of the blog is laid back. Getting a professional logo makes your page look a lot better, and thus, more attractive to your readers.

# Header

The header is the top of the web page you are designing. This is where the title of the page is found or you might want to put your name there. Headers are often where the logo is displayed, and also generally, there are links to different pages on your site. For instance, you might put a link to your eCommerce page. Note that this header is a graphic location on your blog page and not the header where your keywords are stored. Where the keywords are stored is within the code of the web page itself.

# Sidebars

Sidebars are a major part of the blog, and as such, they are highly customizable. The sidebar is found along either side of the blog. The sidebar is fixed and the same for every page of your site.

The sidebar is where a lot of information is stored. Depending on what you want on your site, you can include links to other pages, a Google search for your site, social media share buttons, archive links, or a blogroll, which is a list of blogs you follow or promote. This is where you can put links to other blogs that you have networked with. It is also where you can add third-party software like widgets or plug-ins.

# Footers

The footer is the bottom of the blog and is often used for copyright and/or contact information.

Some very advanced users use this area for other uses, but that is very rare. Since it is so rarely used, if you put anything else in the footer, it could be overlooked by your readers.

## Flare

Flare refers to anything that blinks, flashes, or something that attempts to get the reader's attention. Some flare can be useful, but too much and your readers might be so attracted to the flare that they do not give proper attention to the blog post itself. Suffice to say, a little flair goes a long way. Too much flare can overwhelm your reader and make your page unattractive to potential readers. Flare is usually placed in the sidebar.

## Color and Spacing

Blogging platforms allow you to change the color of the background and text on your blog. This gives you a lot of freedom to customize your page. However, it is very easy to reduce your page's readability. Your blog needs to be easy to read and changing colors often causes the page to be more difficult to read. You should also look out for the text blending into the background. If the text blends in, the page becomes very difficult to read. This also often happens if you have a background graphic that competes with the blog itself.

# Graphics

As discussed earlier, graphics, from logos to other types of artwork, is very important for your blog.

You can get a logo from many different places on the internet. If you are looking for logo creation software, there is a large variety of them available. Just Google "logo creator" and choose one of the software packages that come up in the search results.

If you want to get a professional logo, you can turn to Craig's List and look for graphic designers and artists that create logos or post a job on the site. Logos obtained through Craig's List are typically cheaper, however, they may vary in quality.

Another option is to go to a website that works with freelance artists. Sites like this are similar to the Textbroker service mentioned in Chapter 3. Essentially, there are marketplaces where you can purchase the art from the freelance artist directly. An example of a marketplace site is https://99designs.com. 99designs allows you to interact directly with the artists or you can set up a challenge where designers submit ideas and you can choose from the one you want.

You can get other artwork done for your site as well. For instance, you can get a banner graphic. A banner graphic is similar to a logo but the banner graphic is long and relatively short. You can also get banner graphics done by a professional artist from the avenues as the logo. Banner graphics typically run the length of the web page or the area allowed by the blogging platform you choose to use.

To get the most out of the banner graphic, you can also use it for your forum posts, as banner graphics are the same size as the signature on your profile. You can also use it at the top of your social media profiles and Tweets. Hence, getting a professional banner graphic is very useful and you can use the graphic in many different places.

You can also get other graphics or artwork for your website, depending on what your blog's needs are.

## Link Colors

Another thing you can customize is your link colors. Most blogging software lets you control the color of a link before, during, and after you click the link. Just like text not blending into the background, the link colors should be clear and not blend into the background. When they blend into the background, it makes the page less visually attractive as well as difficult to read.

## WordPress

As mentioned elsewhere, WordPress is the leading software for websites and blogs. With WordPress, you can control most aspects about the page while having the bonus of widgets and plug-ins that you can add to your blog. Note that the difference between a widget and a plug-in is that widgets are built directly into the WordPress software, while plug-ins are third-party software that work with WordPress.

## Themes

The first and most important way to customize your WordPress blog is to use themes. Themes are preset designs with various page layouts including the placement of the blog, placement of the graphics on the page, colors of text and links, and various other visual elements.

There are a very large number of WordPress themes available for download or installation. Because of the variety of themes, you can choose one without worrying that every blog will look like yours.

Themes are very useful because they make it fast and easy to both initially set-up your blog and update it later on as you can install or select another theme and quickly change the settings at any time.

## Other Customization Options

There are many other ways to customize your blog if you are using the WordPress software. The software allows you to change the way that the blog looks and acts. You can add widgets and plug-ins to add functionality to your blog. Just like other blogging platforms, you can control the various aspects of the web page such as font colors and background images. Below is a list of the various customization options.

- **Site Title and Tagline:** This option lets you change your site title and sub-title of your site. The tagline, or subtitle, allows you to add a catchy or informative phrase. The subtitle can help draw your readers to your blog. You can also remove the title and subtitle from your page.

- **Colors:** You can control the color of your header text and background with this option.

- **Header Image:** You can add a picture to your header. This can be a logo, banner graphic, or another image. The size and shape for the graphic vary from theme to theme, so make sure that your graphics work with the theme you have chosen.

- **Background Image:** This feature lets you upload an image for the background instead of a background of a single color. When considering a background image, be sure that your text and link colors do not get blended into the image.

- **Navigation:** After you make a navigation menu, you can create a menu that lets the reader navigate your blog. These menus make moving around your various pages much easier.

- **Widgets:** Widgets are additional options that you can add to your page. These can include search features, archives of your blog posts, and other useful options. Like themes, there are many widgets you can add to your blog.

## Plug-ins

Plug-ins is third-party software that you can use to add to your WordPress site. Like widgets, plug-ins add to the functionality of the blog. There is a large number of plug-ins available for WordPress.

If you're enjoying this book, I would appreciate it if you went to the place of purchase and left a short positive review. Thank you.

# CHAPTER 7: MAKE MONEY WITH YOUR BLOG

One of the major reasons to have a blog is to make money off of it. Monetizing your blog is not difficult and it can give you a steady stream of income. You can also do this passively, which means that you do not have to continue to do something in order for it to keep generating money for you. For example, if you have advertisements on your page, you do not have to do anything for those ads to make money for you. All you need to do is to keep posting and making sure that your blog is a leader in your subject.

This chapter will discuss methods that you can use to generate income from your blog including affiliate markets, using advertisements, sponsorships, and by having virtual summits. These methods give you several ways to monetize your blog and make real money off of it.

## Affiliate Markets

Affiliate markets are where you have a link to products that readers can purchase. These products are made by a third-party that you have an agreement with, and for every product that you sell for the affiliate, you get paid some of the money. This is a great way to monetize your blog, since all you need to do is prepare the page for the affiliate products, and the affiliate might give you content that is already ready to go on your site.

Once you have the link set up, you can sit back and wait while the sales come in. You can also have many different affiliates on your web page with each one potentially generating income for you.

Typically, with affiliate markets, you need to make sure that the products match your blog. It can be confusing if you have products that do not match your subject matter. For instance, if you have a comic book blog, it doesn't make much sense for you to have a fitness product linked to it. Optimally, your target audience should be likely to purchase from your affiliates, otherwise, the sales might distract from your blog and confuse your readers.

Affiliate markets are a great way to start generating income when you first start your blog and before you have started selling your own products (see Chapter 8).

Some affiliate markets you might want to check out are Amazon Associates, ClickBank, or LinkShare.

## Advertising

Another way you can make money off of your blog is by putting advertising on your blog. You can add many different types of ads. Essentially, you can get paid to put the ads on your page.

There are two types of ads that you can add to your web page. They are PPC (pay-per-click) and display ads. PPC ads are ones where you get paid for each ad that your reader clicks. Display ads, on the other hand, just display on the web page. You can even combine the two types of ads and have both on your blog.

One place that you can get ads for your blog is Google AdSense. Google AdSense is an ad program that Google runs. It lets you add both PPC and display ads to your website. Once the ads are ready, you do not have to continue to do anything. Google will update the ads and will pay you for having the ads on your page.

Advertising services like Google AdSense sound like a great way to generate income, however, the truth of the situation is if you don't have a lot of traffic, the amount of money you will make off of the advertising will be negligible. To have successful ads, you really need to have around 10,000 views or clicks per day.

When you first start out your blog, having ads is probably not the best option, and it might not be worth the time it takes to set up. It is also worth noting that not all blogging platforms allow you to add ads to their pages, so depending on where you are hosting your site, ads may not even be an option.

## Email Marketing

Another option for monetizing your blog is to use your email list for email marketing. Email marketing is when you send links and ways to purchase things through your email list of your readers. Email marketing can be very lucrative.

You can send emails that include products you produce on your own or you can send links to affiliate products. You can bundle these emails along with the other email that you are sending out. For instance, you might send out an email with your latest update as well as a link to an affiliate product.

Email marketing is a very powerful way to monetize your blog. The larger your email list is, the more chance you have for your email marketing to pay off, so if you want to do email marketing you will want to build your list.

There are professional email list services that are available. These services help you to keep track of your emails and your list without having to spend a lot of time maintaining them. These include popular email marketing platforms like ConvertKit or InfusionSoft. With these email marketing tools, you can estimate that you will make $1 per subscriber per month.

## Sponsorships

Another way to make money off of your blog is to get sponsorships. A sponsorship is when you have another website sponsor your page, essentially paying you to post your content. You can make a decent amount off of sponsorships. However, you should have a good amount of traffic before you get a page sponsored. Sponsored pages are generally easy to construct as the page that is sponsoring you will generally let you know what content they want on the page.

It is also important to be upfront that the page is sponsored. If you are not clear about that, it can cost you, as the FTC fines people that have sponsored pages but do not list it as such. Sponsored pages are not considered as organic as a page that you write for yourself without sponsorship. In fact, Google will rank your page and the sponsoring page if it is discovered that you have a sponsored page, but you do not disclose it. Many on the web find it highly unethical if you do not disclose that it is a sponsored page, and readers may think you are trying to trick them or that you only have the blog to make money and do not care about them. This means that your page will lose the trust of your readers, and from past chapters, it should be clear that you need the trust between yourself as the blogger and your readers or viewers.

## Paid Reviews

Posting paid reviews is another way to make money off of your blog. With paid reviews, companies send you their products or services and you review them on your blog. With paid reviews, the company with the product sends it to you and has you try the product or service out. The products you get sent can range from electronics, video games, online services, and other items. The company that produced the product then pays you to review the product or service on your blog. Once you have tried the product out, you can create a blog post with what you think about the product including the pros and cons. You can even compare several items in order to show what is the best product, and why you should purchase that one.

## Virtual Summits

Another way to make money off of your blog is to host a virtual summit. A virtual summit is where you get a group of experts together for a panel and a discussion on a subject. You can create a video of the panel and post it to your blog. This video should be highly informative or even humorous. The video should be compelling in order to draw your readers and viewers in. You can create the video using chat programs such as Skype, Google Hangouts, or another video conferencing software.

If you don't know where to look, it can be difficult to find experts to be on your panel. However, there is a wealth of great experts out there just waiting for an invitation. A good place to look for experts is your fellow bloggers. At this point in your blog, you should already have networked with several bloggers that you can invite onto your panel. If you are networking on the subject of your blog, you should already have several contacts that are in the same vein as your blog. This cross-promotion allows not only you to use the virtual summit video, but you can also make it available to the other bloggers. The other bloggers can post links back to your own blog. Hence, the video can be good for all of the bloggers involved.

You might ask yourself how you can make money off of a virtual summit. The answer is to charge for the video of experts. You can charge for each individual video or you can offer an all-access pass that gives the reader or viewer full access to all of your summit videos. To draw attention to your blog, you can even offer the videos for free for a limited time such as 24 or 48 hours. After that initial time, it costs to view the video.

# CHAPTER 8: SELLING YOUR OWN PRODUCTS

One of the best ways to monetize your blog is to make your own products or services to sell either through your own eCommerce store or by selling them through Amazon. To do this, you just need to create the products and make them available for sale. You can sell your products through blog posts, e-mail marketing, your social media posts, or through your eCommerce store.

This chapter will discuss some of the various products you can create and sell from your blog.

## ecommerce Solutions

Before you can sell your products, you first need an eCommerce store in order to sell them. The easiest way to set up an eCommerce store is through your website hosting service. While not all hosting sites offer eCommerce stores, especially the free ones like Blogger, many of the hosting options do offer eCommerce solutions. Typically, you have to have a paid subscription to a site like Weebly or Wix in order to set up the store. Setting up an eCommerce store can be confusing, but your hosting sites offer support for their services, so if you have any difficulty setting up the store, you should contact them for help.

In order to have an eCommerce store, you need a merchant ID. Once you have a merchant ID and your eCommerce store set up, you can begin selling your products on your blog. Typically, you get a merchant ID from your web hosting site when you purchase the site's tools for eCommerce solutions. With a merchant ID, you can begin taking credit and debit card orders for your products and/or services. Another place you can get a merchant ID is through PayPal. PayPal offers eCommerce solutions using its payment processing network.

## Selling eBooks

One of the easiest products to produce and sell is eBooks. To sell an eBook, all you have to do write it, format it and put it on your eCommerce store as a download. You can set your price to whatever you want it to be, and you can sell it either through your own eCommerce store or via Amazon. Amazon has a thriving eBook market, and putting your eBook on Amazon has the added bonus that potential customers, who are not readers of your blog, can be exposed to your book. This potentially expands your customer base without them having to find your blog. You can also gain blog followers based on how informative and helpful your book is. To write an eBook, you need to pick a subject associated with your blog. The book should be focused and informative on the subject and needs to be free of grammatical and spelling errors.

## Selling Courses

Another electronic product that you can create is a course. A course is a step-by-step instruction manual. Courses are often in a slide-show format so that it is easy to move from one screen to another. You can sell courses for most subjects, but like eBooks, it will sell off your blog if it is associated with it in some way. An example of a course is a nutrition course for a fitness blog. For example, you may have sections on basic nutrition, portion sizes, and the positive effects of exercise on the body. You can also separate related subjects into multiple courses or you can have a series of courses where each one builds off the others.

## Coaching

One very lucrative service you can offer is coaching. Coaching services are where you stay in contact with your clients in order to assist them with an aspect of their life. Popular coaching services include life coaching, business development coaching, or career coach.

In order to be a coach, you should be very familiar with the subject you are coaching about. You should be very informative and an asset to your coaching clients. One way to do this is to coach about the same subject as your blog. This makes it easy for you to hook new clients because they can see what you have already written about the subject.

One of the really great things about selling coaching is that you can make a large amount of money with only a handful of clients. Having relatively few clients also allows you to have the time to work with each of them in one-on-one interactions.

When setting up your coaching services, you set up various packages with different services that your clients can purchase. You should also be very clear about what you are offering with each package. It is also important when selling coaching services to make the process very easy. Instead, coaching should be very simple and easy to purchase.

## Physical Products

Not only can you sell electronic products, but you can also sell physical products. Physical products are a more concrete purchase as the customer gets a physical object, and not just an eBook or a course. The physical products you sell can be almost anything. Some items you can sell are coasters, mugs, stickers, t-shirts, prints, and many other products. You can place your logo or any other artwork you have on your products, which helps solidify the brand associated with your blog. Below are some very common items that you can sell. You can even make bundles where you sell several items at once.

Physical items are also good for contests.

- **T-Shirts:** Perhaps the best physical product to sell is t-shirts. T-shirts are not just easy and cheap to produce, but they are very easy to tie into your blog. This is an item that is very good for having logos and art, and because you can put a link to your site on them, they can even become good marketing to people who have seen the shirt but have not yet been exposed to your blog. If you are selling coaching services, you can easily tie the shirt into those services with an inspirational quote.

- **Stickers:** Stickers are another great product to sell or give away. Stickers are useful because they can be placed on a multitude of items such as on guitars, cars, or on a laptop.

# CONCLUSION

Thanks for making it through to the end of *Blogging: For profit, passive income idea for making money working from home*. Let's hope it was informative and able to provide you with all of the tools you need to achieve your goals whatever they may be. Now that you have finished it, you can take the information from this book and make your own blog and so that you can begin to monetize it.

The next step is to stop reading so you can begin creating your blog. Using the information from this book will help propel you to the top of the blogging charts. Even before you are popular, you can make an eCommerce store, write your first eBooks, and create courses for your clients and readers.

Complex tasks are best completed when you break them down into smaller parts. An important aspect of any writing or producing is to set deadlines for yourself. Setting deadlines for yourself can help you to complete your blog easily and quickly. Setting individual deadlines helps keep you writing and creating. This will help you to meet your goals so that you can make the best blog you can.

Finally, thank you for reading this book and may all your goals and dreams come true. If you've enjoyed this book, I would appreciate it if you went to the place of purchase and left a short positive review. Thank you.

# DROPSHIPPING

*How to generate passive income using e-commerce advanced strategies, Shopify, Amazon FBA and eBay*

**Gary Loomer**

# TABLE OF CONTENTS

# INTRODUCTION

I want to congratulate you for downloading this book. We live in a time and age where online business opportunities and business models are proliferating, and it would be great for us to dip our fingers to try and tap into some of this wealth. This was one of the reasons why this book was written, to help you make money online using this simple method: Drop shipping.

All the chapters in this book will cover everything you need to know about dropshipping. In the first chapter, we will discuss what the whole dropshipping business model is and how it works. The second chapter will discuss how to start your very own dropshipping business by examining the top websites for dropshipping and the upfront investment on each website. We will then talk about the pros and cons of each website. The third chapter will explain how to find the most profitable niche so you can make the most profits and gain some of that wealth. The fourth chapter will talk about how to find the right supplier and how to build a great relationship with them. The fifth chapter will introduce a step by step process in order to find the most profitable product to sell which will make you the most profits. In the final chapter, we will discuss how to get targeted traffic using Facebook, Instagram and other methods so you can start to increase those sales.

I know there are plenty of books on this subject, and I would like to thank you for choosing this particular one. I know this book will offer you the knowledge you need to get started on dropshipping the right way.

# Chapter 1: What is Dropshipping?

Ok, so now on to the big burning question. What is dropshipping? Well simply put, dropshipping is a business model where you are going to act as the "middle man." So mainly what you are going to do is find a product from a supplier at a really low price. And thereafter for this product, you make an online store or sell on an online store. One way or another you will need a storefront from where you can display your products, sell and collect payments. On this storefront, you would upload compelling product photos and description.

On your store or website, you will sell the product at a much higher price than the price you will be paying for it. You then target your store to specific groups of people who will be interested in purchasing your product. Once they buy the product from you, you will then go to your supplier and buy it,  and directly ship it to the buyer without you even touching the product. This leaves you with the profit in your pocket.

Now that you have a basic introduction to what dropshipping is, let me talk to you about the benefits of dropshipping compared to other business models. There are a lot of benefits to doing a dropshipping style of business.  The main one is that you will not be holding any kind of inventory. This means you won't have to make any big upfront investments in buying a whole lot of products or renting out a warehouse where you have to store it. Another great benefit with this style of business model is that you will not have to worry about shipping the product. The supplier will take care of that for you. Sometimes depending on where you shop the product from, the supplier may even take care of the customer services side of things. This may also include refunds, late delivery etc.

Ths may feel like a surprise for some of us, as we have this notion that to set up an import/export business or retail business you need to have significant upfront investments and a big storage place where you can keep all your products. Well, I am here to tell you that those days are long gone. The truth is that you don't need a whole lot of upfront investment to start your very own business, all you need is a laptop or a computer, a high-quality product which you can get for cheap, a storefront and an audience. No large upfront investment, no warehouse to rent, nothing! This is why dropshipping is one of the best business models and has so much potential to give back great rewards.

There are two ways you can go about starting your dropshipping business which we will cover in-depth within this chapter. The first way is online dropshipping. This is your typical way of dropshipping which is done by most people when they first start their dropshipping business. The second one is warehouse dropshipping. Although it requires a little more upfront investment, it still has a lot of benefits to it. Let's dive deep into these two dropshipping methods.

## Online dropshipping

Online dropshipping is one the most common ways people decide to start up their dropshipping business these days. This is the method which comes to mind when people talk about dropshipping. In this method you will have to find a supplier who can provide you with high-quality products for a cheap price. One thing you have to make sure when finding your supplier is that they will have the ability to deliver the product for you directly to the buyer without you having to being involved (Otherwise the customer management headache you will have to face, may not be worth using this method). Using this method, you will most likely have to make your own website like using Shopify to make your online store, or if you don't want to create your website you can use sites like eBay, Amazon marketplace, etc. We will discuss later in this book which websites to choose for your dropshipping business.

Now, if you decide to use this method for your dropshipping you will have to make sure that you have a safe and secure way of collecting payments from your client. Not only will it help you get paid safely, but it will also make your costumers feel safe once they decide to make a purchase on your website or product. If you are thinking about creating your own e-commerce website for your products, then make sure you add a trust badge on your website to help customers feel safe whilst using your site. Ensure you do research into a secure payment gateway to apply for your website. If you're using Shopify as your website, you will not need to worry about trust as the website already has security on the site. Another great tip is to have a PayPal account, as many people use PayPal to make purchases on your website. So if you want to get paid, make a PayPal account.

Now, I want to discuss the benefits of using online dropshipping for your business. Like I mentioned before, you don't have to hold any inventory, meaning there's no need to buy any products in bulk or rent out a warehouse where you can store your products. All you are simply going to do is make a website, upload the product on your website with a markup and once someone purchases the product you will simply give the shipping information to your supplier and he or she will mail it out to them! Plain and simple. The only thing you might need an investment in would be buying a domain name for your website, which I highly recommend. Domain costs are reasonable and would probably cost you around $10 a year. Also if you are not a programmer or can't code, then you may have to use a website platform to start selling your products and to collect payments, which will cost you additionally $30 to $120 a month (depending on which website platform you decide to use). If you want, you can pay for the whole year in one go with your website provider, which will save you money.

Just like any business model, there can be some challenges to this method so it would be a good idea to address them. The main one is shipping times.  We live in a world where some companies ship products within a day or ordering. Most of the time the supplier you will be working with will be from China, so the orders for your clients will be shipped out of China. For you to actually make a profit on your sale you will have to use the most cost efficient way of shipping, which will result in slower shipping times. Now this isn't a total deal breaker, but people are impatient, some more than others. So if you don't pick the right supplier and shipping methods, you can expect to get cancellations as people will not be happy with the delays in delivery. Not all your orders will get refunded, but some may.  It's unrealistic to expect shipping times of one day like some of your competitors offer as they are large cooperatives with an established infrastructure. However, I will give some tips and techniques to get faster delivery to your client using dropshipping, later in the book.

Another drawback with this business model is that you won't be able to determine the quality of the products which you're going to be selling, not unless you buy them for yourself first, which I would recommend you do before putting them into your store. This will lower the risk of your products getting refunded for quality issues. One more thing you need to consider is driving traffic to your product. Since you won't be affiliated with any big companies, you will have to drive traffic to your own website or storefront using paid advertisements.

## Warehouse dropshipping

In this method, you will have to buy a certain quantity of products upfront. And as you have these products with you, you have the benefit of faster shipping, which will allow you to have fewer chances of cancellations and have better customer satisfaction, which is different from the online dropshipping method.

So, let's dwell on how warehouse dropshipping exactly works. The first thing to remember is that you will be selling your product on a website like Amazon. You can still use the warehouse dropshipping method with your own website but you will have to rent out a warehouse, and shipping would be your responsibility. Companies like Amazon will let you store products in their warehouse and ship the products out for you, which is why it is recommended to work with a big company when doing a warehouse dropshipping model. You find a product for cheap or buy it from a warehouse in bulk, then you will ship your inventory to the company's warehouse. Once that is done you can sit back and see the profits in your bank account; you don't have to worry about anything like customer service, making a website, or capturing a payment-- nothing! The company will take care of everything for you.

But, the upfront investment to start this business model is higher than online dropshipping. Let me break it down for you. Depending on the product and how much of it you buy, you are looking to spend $1,000 to $2,000 on your inventory. Companies also charge you to have a seller's account. That could start from around $39.99 and go up depending on how many products you sell, plus a fee for every product shipped. So as you can see, there is quite a bit more upfront investment compared to the online dropshipping method. Although this method has a big upfront investment it also has some positives to consider.

There are a lot of benefits with this dropshipping method, so let us talk about them. The best benefit by using this dropshipping method is that you can actually quality check the products before you decide to sell them. It is important that you check your product quality before you ship them off in order for your refund rates to be low. Another great benefit with warehouse dropshipping is that, once you have shipped it to the company warehouse, you don't have to worry about anything else. The company will take care of the shipping, etc. Another huge benefit with this business model is that you will not have to worry about advertising your product as much as the online dropshipping method. Since your product will be listed in the company website, which already gets a lot of traffic, you won't have to worry about promoting your product too much, which could mean less paid advertisement and more money in your pocket.

All that being said, there is one major flaw with this method of dropshipping. There is no guarantee all your products will sell, if any. Even though you will be listing your product on a website which gets a lot of traffic, it won't always equate to sales. Remember there will be a lot of products you will be competing with on the website, so making sure your product sells is crucial if you don't want to lose your investment.

So hopefully, you now know what dropshipping is and the different ways you can go about starting your dropshipping business. If you are still confused, then don't worry. Keep reading, and it will start to get less confusing as we go along in this book, and hopefully, everyone reading this book now has an understanding on what it takes to start a dropshipping business. In my opinion, dropshipping is one of the most straightforward business models to scale up and make money on, so keep on reading.

# CHAPTER 2: HOW TO START A DROPSHIPPING BUSINESS

Now, since you now have an idea on the types of dropshipping business models and a rough idea on how to go about starting your own dropshipping business, I would really like to get into the specifics of starting your very own dropshipping business. Now, if you have been doing some research online on dropshipping, you might have heard of a lot of websites where you can start your dropshipping business, but for this chapter, we will stick with the top three websites. Those three would be Shopify, Amazon,and eBay.

The reason why we will be only going through these three websites is that every other dropshipping platform is mimicking these three websites, so there's no need to worry about learning each dropshipping website, as they are similar to the top three. We will go into details on each of the websites, we will discuss things such as the exact startup cost of each website, how to get paid on each website and how much legwork it will take to get started on each website. One more thing I would really like to talk about is the potential income with each website, as there are a lot of misconceptions floating around the internet regarding this topic, so I will be covering that as well. Let's start by going through the website which popularized the whole dropshipping business model, which is Shopify.

# Shopify

So for people who don't know what Shopify is, Shopify is an e-commerce company founded in Canada. What Shopify provides is an e-commerce platform or an online store for its users. It was originally founded by Scott Lake, Daniel Weinard, and the current CEO, Tobias Lutke. Essentially what Shopify provides you with is a secure online store where you can sell products to consumers online. Most people use this website for online dropshipping rather than warehouse dropshipping since Shopify does not provide users with a warehouse. Starting your very own dropshipping business using Shopify as your platform is very easy and cost effective compared to other platforms.

To start making money with dropshipping using Shopify as your platform, all you will need is a supplier which can ship out the products anywhere in the world for cheap. That's it for the requirements; now I want to get specific with the start-up cost of getting started with Shopify as it is not free, but it is really cost efficient compared to other business models out there.

Now first things first, you will need to buy a domain name. You really need to make sure that your website looks trustworthy, and for that to happen you will need a domain name. Buying a domain name is inexpensive; it will only cost you around $10 to $25 USD per year, depending on the domain name. Now once you get that sorted, you will now have to sign up on Shopify. Since Shopify offers a free 14-day trial, I would recommend you make sure that the store name or brand you decide upon is not taken before you buy a domain name for your website or store. Once you have decided your store name, etc. , it will now be time to buy a package from Shopify which will allow you to start selling your products. Shopify offers three packages, which include

Basic Shopify package ($29.99 USD a month)

Shopify package ($79.99 USD a month)

Advanced Shopify package ($299.99 USD a month)

Also note, if you want to save money you can buy these packages upfront on a yearly basis. But that's totally up to you.

Now you might be wondering which one to get started with. Let me explain each of them to you. If you're just starting your dropshipping business I would like to say right off the bat that you don't need the advanced Shopify package. Once you have your business rolling and if you want to expand, you can do your research on it and upgrade, but for starters, just pick between the basic Shopify package or the Shopify package. If your funds are low, and you want to start making money online then you can totally start off with the basic package, but if you have some extra cash to spare then I would recommend upgrading to the Shopify package as it has some useful benefits.

The useful benefit this Shopify package provides you with, compared to the basic Shopify package, is the lower amount of online credit card rates compared to the basic Shopify package. Even though it's minuscule, it adds up once you start making over thousands of dollars a month. Another great benefit of using the Shopify package compared to the basic Shopify package is that you can start making your own gift cards. As you know, in order to make sales on this platform you will need to get some traffic first before you can actually make some sales online. So having these small incentives can add up to more sales in the future. Other than that these packages are identical. If you will be using Shopify for online dropshipping purposes, you can go with either package which fits your budget. It is up to you which one you want to get started with.

One more thing you can invest in to really make your store stand out are logos, which you will need for your Shopify store. You can get them done professionally by hiring someone on fiverr.com. The logo will not cost you more than $25 USD to get started. If you're able to, you could create the logo yourself, so you wouldn't need to hire someone to make it. Canvas.com is a great tool you could use to make your free logo.

To give a summary of costs so far, to get started with dropshipping using Shopify:

Shopify package $29.99 or $79.99 USD

Domain name $ 10 to $20 USD

Logo around $25 if using someone, otherwise free if created by yourself.


So to get started with Shopify it will cost you $35/45 + $29.99 USD every month

after that, if you go for the cheapest option, or $35/45 + $79.99 every month after that for the next option. Regardless, the costs are not astronomical.


Now, let's talk about the work you will have to put in for your Shopify business to flourish. You will have to make sure your website looks presentable. Shopify provides you with some great themes which can be used to build up your website, no problem. But it does require some work to be put in. Other things you will have to take care of are customer inquiries and complaints. Since it is your brand and company, you will have to deal with everything from complaints to fulfilling an order. So make sure you have an email created for your store inquiries. Also, like I said before, you will have to put emphasis on getting traffic, since no one will know about your store except your family and friends. Other than that, you should be fine.

How you get paid on Shopify is simple as well; all you have to do is make a PayPal account, since some people might choose to complete their transaction using PayPal. Also, Shopify will make you put in your banking information, for the others who use a credit card to make a purchase at your store. Shopify will directly deposit into your account.

The final thing I would like to discuss is how much you can realistically make using Shopify and the online dropshipping method. Since it is your brand and your company, you can make as much as you want. You can become a millionaire or a billionaire with this method, as long as you build a following for your business, which again will be talked about in the later chapters. Overall, the sky is the limit! Work hard and be patient, and you will get what you desire.

## Amazon FBA

Unless you have been living under a rock, you know that Amazon is one of the biggest e-commerce companies in the world, with its founder and owner's net worth being a whopping $150 billion dollars, making him the richest man in the world. Jeff Bezos founded his company in the early 90s; his goal was to sell books online. Now Amazon sells everything you can think of. Amazon is the biggest e-commerce company in the world and its website has one of the highest amounts of online traffic in the world. Needless to say, working with Amazon could make you money.

Now you might be wondering, what does the FBA stand for? It stands for Fulfillment By Amazon.

What you have to do in order to a part of this program is simple. First find a product which you can get for cheap, secondly, buy it in bulk, and finally, the third is to ship it to Amazon's warehouse, where it can be shipped off to the customer. It's that simple. Now, the startup cost with this business model is a little bit higher, so let's break it down:

Buying products in bulk for cheap: $1000 - $3000 USD

If you sell more than 40 items a month you will have to pay $39.99

So, on the lower end, you can get started for $1000 USD to $3000 USD plus $39.99 a month if you sell more than 40 products. Plus there is a charge for each product they ship out, but don't worry, it will only be charged once someone orders a product.

Even though there is a bigger upfront investment in this type of dropshipping, it still has some benefits. For example, since your products will be listed on Amazon, you will already be getting free traffic, which would equal higher chances of a sale. Unlike Shopify, Amazon takes care of the back end, like customer refunds, questions, etc. All you do is get the product, ship it to Amazon's warehouse and you will start earning money.

Now let's talk about the work you will have to do in order to get this business started from the ground up. The first thing is finding a cheap supplier. For you to actually make some profits you will have to find products at a low cost. Second, buy it in bulk, and third, ship it to Amazon's warehouse. When business takes off all you will have to worry about is restocking your products by shipping them to Amazon so you can make more money; that's all the work you will have to do. Like I said, all the back end stuff Amazon will take care of, such as shipping, customer service, etc.

So let's talk about how you will get paid on Amazon FBA. It's simple, similar to Shopify. You will first have to make a seller's account on Amazon, and once that is done you will add your banking information to the account. Amazon will pay you the profits you make right into your bank account and you don't have to worry about anything else, besides filing your taxes.

The final thing I would like to talk about is income, how much can you make on Amazon FBA. Since AmazonFBA is not a personal brand which you can grow the income will be limited. I know the top earners can make over two million a year using Amazon FBA, which for some can be amazing to see this kind of cash. But for others who really want to build their brand, Amazon FBA would not be the answer. Now the benefit with this business model is that if you do everything right, you can make money faster and you could scale up higher, but there is a tap on the amount of money you can make here.

# eBay

eBay is one the most successful e-commerce websites, founded in 1995 by Pierre Omidyar. It has quickly become a household name around the world.  What started as a bidding website online has now become one of the most popular places to sell your items, and it also can be used with great success for drop-shippers all around the world.

Now, starting up with eBay as a dropshipper would probably be the cheapest way to go about it. To get started, all you will need is a supplier who can provide you with cheap products, and a PayPal account to accept payments. There are literally no upfront costs to get started, and you can use the images suppliers have on their pages and upload them to your eBay account. The way eBay makes money is through transactions; once someone purchases a product from you, eBay will take a cut out of that purchase, plain and simple. So to get started with eBay you will need $0 and a cheap connection for your products.

I know, eBay sounds like the best option out of the three right now, but there are some major flaws. The first one is you can't build a brand like you can on Shopify.  You see, what appeals to most people is trying out a new brand and seeing what they like. With eBay, it's like buying something for really cheap and on sale, so it will be hard to mark up your products at a higher price like you can on Amazon and Shopify, which will equal fewer profits. Another major problem I see with this method is that it is competing with Amazon, which already has a bigger following and is more trusted by people. So with that in mind, getting organic traffic like you would on Amazon would be hard. So I would recommend spending some money on ads if you want to get sales on eBay. Since the competition on eBay is so high, it will make it really hard for your product to organically sell.

With all that being said, let's talk about how you will be paid on eBay. You will be paid through PayPal, so make sure you have your PayPal account set up. But don't forget eBay will take some money out of the transaction online, plus so will PayPal. So keep that in mind as you move forward.

For everyone who wants to get started with eBay, don't worry, as there is some money to be made. eBay dropshippers can make $1,000 to $3,000 USD as a side income every month, which isn't bad at all, but you can't expect to become a millionaire through eBay. So if you are looking to make a side income, then eBay can definitely fulfill that for you for with no start-up cost.

Now, it's your choice to pick out which website and dropshipping method you want to continue with in starting your own dropshipping business. I know all three of these websites have some amazing benefits but they also come with some issues. For you to find out which type of dropshipping business you want to start with is simple. First ask yourself how much money can you invest, second, ask yourself how much money do you want to make, and then third, how much of this income do you want it to be passive, meaning you don't do a lot of work and you make profits. Now if you have money to invest and want to see returns quickly and have it be passive, then Amazon FBA would be the right fit for you. If your goal is to start your own company and build your own brand, while making amazing amounts of money, then Shopify would be the answer for you. Finally, if you want to make money but you don't have money to invest, then I would highly recommend eBay so you can start earning some side income quickly.

With that being said, I hope this chapter really opened your mind to the different ideas of dropshipping and how much you can make. Like I said, it is up to you to decide on picking the right business model for your needs. It's time for you to evaluate your situation and come up with a business plan that works for you. All three websites can make you money, some more than the others, but again there is a price to pay for each of the websites, so choose wisely.

If you're enjoying this book, I would appreciate it if you went to the place of purchase and left a short positive review. Thank you

# CHAPTER 3: MOST PROFITABLE NICHE

So, hopefully, by now, you have decided on which type of dropshipping method and which website you will be moving forward with. Regardless of whichever method you choose, you will need to make sure that your products sell, for you to actually make money. So how will you actually sell products? Well, simply by finding a niche which already has customers and not enough products for all. Here's the cold truth, you will not sell anything or make any money if what you're selling does not have a demand for it. This is why choosing the right niche is imperative for your success in the dropshipping business.

Now, most of you might be wondering what a niche is. Well, to explain it in the most simple manner, a niche is something relating to or being a part of a certain product or service, etc. So, for example, selling something like a dog bracelet to dog lovers, that would be considered a niche. So, as you can see, having a niche to sell in is imperative for your success in this dropshipping business. So in this chapter, what I really want to talk about is how can you find a profitable niche where you can make some amazing profits, without wasting money on buying your products in bulk and letting it sit in the warehouse or paying monthly fees and spending money on advertisements without seeing any profits.

So from my experience with Amazon, Shopify and eBay, when you first initially start you won't be able to make a lot of money in niches which are saturated or have a lot of products to sell. These companies or people will have a lot of money invested in advertisements, and our goal is to get started with minimal money and slowly scale up. The ideal situation for you to make money is to be a big fish in a small pond rather than a small fish in a big pond. Your job is to find a profitable niche which hasn't been tapped into, but you know has potential to sell and make you money.

So to find out a niche which will actually sell and make you money, I have created two ways, or rather I should say two techniques, to find a niche and make money online. So let me first show the websites I use to find a niche which will actually help you make money. The first website I use is Amazon; it is one of the biggest e-commerce websites. So anything that sells well on Amazon will sell anywhere. The second one is Facebook groups and Instagram pages. To find out what you could sell online these pages will help you tremendously. Now let us go into the depths of each way to find a profitable niche. We will begin with Amazon.

## Amazon

As we know by now, Amazon is the biggest online store right now. So whatever sells on Amazon sells anywhere, so if your goal is to find a niche which will make you money and is profitable, then you need to review Amazons products.

If you have been to Amazon's website to purchase a product, or anything for that matter, below you will see the best sellers rank under the product description. What that best seller ranks symbolizes is how much of the product is being bought. This is very important for you to note. If the product is not selling on Amazon, which is the biggest e-commerce store in the world, it will not sell anywhere. Now here is what you are going to do in order to find a product that sells.

The very first thing you are going to do is get on your computer and go to Amazon's website. Now what I want you to do is go on to the best sellers page on Amazon. This page will give you a rough idea on what sells and what doesn't, and also will show you the niche products which are selling already. Anything in the Amazon's best sellers page will most likely sell, that is if you can offer it at a cheaper price. Regardless of which platform you will be using for your dropshipping business, if Amazon has the same product for sale that you do, it will have it for the same price or cheaper than you will. This is the case most of the time, but if you can sell it cheaper than your competitors, meaning Amazon, then you have a winning product! Congrats.

Now if that's not the case, it is time to find an untapped niche. So go to the best sellers page on Amazon and look at the top 100 on that list carefully.  If you see similar products from the same niche, then this niche is profitable. But it could be hard to penetrate into that specific market or niche.  This is where we find a micro-niche. So for example, if the niche is iPhone accessories and there are multiple iPhone accessories on the best sellers list, what we will do is search up iPhone accessories on the Amazon search bar. Then we will go through the top six products and check to see their best sellers list.  If the best sellers list showcases a number below 50,000  for all six items, then this niche is profitable.

Hypothetically, you can sell in this niche and make some great profits. But if the competition is high, then there are fewer chances of you actually making profits, so if you want to make sure the completion is low, look at the search engine number. If the search engine number has a number lower than 5,000 items, then the niche is small, and if the top six products have a ranking of lower than 50,000 on the best sellers ranking, then you have a winning product and a niche to get into. So, if you search up iPhone accessories and it has 20,000 items for sale, it would be harder for you tap into, but on the other hand, if you search up iPhone phone cases and it has fewer than 5,000 items for sale and the top six items best seller rank is lower than 50,000, we have a winner at hand. So this is how you use Amazon to find a profitable niche.

# Facebook groups and Instagram pages

This is another place where you can find niches to sell in. A lot of Facebook pages and Instagram pages are made to share videos and content online for people to look at, simply because they are a big fan of it. They have a special connection to this niche for some reason; it could be personal, who knows. But you can use this fan page or groups to offer them something they can't refuse.

Think about it, if you were a big fan of dogs and you loved dogs. Wouldn't you want to buy a $25 t-shirt which says "I Love Dogs"? Of course you would, because you are a super-fan. Now the best part about this method is that the people you will advertise your product to will most likely buy it, and there are a lot of pages online where there is a big following but no products to sell. So in order to find these pages, all you will have to do is search and think outside the box, as there are some pages waiting to be sold "I Love something" t-shirts. So look around and search, and once you find your niche, you will making some serious profits.

With all that being said, let me share with you some niches which have made me money in the past:

   Dog lovers

   Cat lovers

   Lion lovers

Car lovers

Electronic accessories

These niches are still quite profitable, so do your research, and if you like them, you can sell on these specific niches.

To finish off this chapter, I would just like to remind you how important finding the right niche is. A niche will either make your business or break it, so if you don't do your research before you decide to sell your products online, then you will regret it. Make sure you use the techniques I taught to find the right niches to sell on, and also feel free to use the niches I have personally made money on, as they could make you some money as well. Now, go online and start researching and find the niche you will be selling on.

# CHAPTER 4: FINDING SUPPLIERS/WHOLESALERS FOR YOUR BUSINESS

Finding the right supplier or the right wholesalers for your dropshipping business is imperative, meaning that you can't "cheap out" or not care about this aspect. As you can imagine, your business will revolve around your supplier quite heavily. Truth be told, if you don't have any products that you can sell, then it would honestly be impossible for you to make any money, which would therefore be equal to no profits. On the other hand, if you decide to "cheap out" and sell low-quality products, chances are, people will return the products. Even though we discussed the importance of finding a proper niche, to the importance of advertising the product the right way, etc., it can't be overridden by an unreliable or a cheap low-quality product.

Finding the right supplier for your dropshipping business purposes is imperative, for both quality purposes and shipping purposes. Now if you are going to be using Amazon FBA or a similar type of dropshipping method, then shipping times do matter in order for you to stock up your products, but it isn't the biggest deal for that dropshipping model compared to dropshipping methods using Shopify. Now with all that being said, quality is the biggest factor you have to worry about when selling your products. So now we will go through the top websites, from where you can find great suppliers for your business. We will also talk about how to build a great relationship with them, and finally, for everyone dropshipping using the method of online dropshipping, I will reveal a secret to getting the fastest shipping anywhere in the world, so your customers stay happy and fewer refunds are being made.

We will break this chapter into two phases. First, we will talk about how to find suppliers for people using online dropshipping. We will go through everything from finding the product, building a relationship with the seller, getting it shipped fast and of course making sure the product is of a high quality. Then we will talk about finding a supplier or a wholesaler for the warehouse dropshipping method. So with that being said, we begin with online dropshipping.

## Online Dropshipping

So, finding a supplier for people using online dropshipping as their business model could be challenging. Since most of the time you will be going by assumptions, what our job with this process is, is to take out as much of the guesswork as we can and find the winning supplier which we are looking for. Now, there are a lot of websites online where you can find products for cheap. But from my experience, AliExpress has one of the best quality product and shipping times. If you have been doing some research online you might have heard things like, "AliExpress is dead," or things of that nature. But I am here to tell you that AliExpress still works amazingly and will help you make some serious profits online. There are some tips and techniques you need to know before you fully start using AliExpress as your sole supplier.

Now, if you don't know what AliExpress is, then let me clarify it for you. Think of AliExpress as the Amazon of China. There are a lot of people selling products online on this website, mostly from China, and as we know most of the products are manufactured in China, meaning the mark up on the products would be a lot less. This means you can easily sell it online for a higher price in the North American market, and to make things even better, the products on AliExpress are mostly similar types of products which are sold or are popular in the North American market. The point I am trying to make is this:  people selling on AliExpress are selling to people specifically who want to start their own dropshipping business.

There are some guidelines you need to follow before you start to use AliExpress to dropship products from, as there are some flaws. The things we need to look into before we start selling products using AliExpress are these:


Supplier review

Product photo's and description

E-packet

How many orders sold

Now, if all these points check out, then your supplier is good. So let's begin with the supplier review. To find out if the supplier is good, the first thing you will need to do is check the reviews. Make sure the reviews on their store are at least 95% positive.  If that's not the case, then either the product quality isn't good or the product is something else when it gets delivered.  Other things to worry about are photos and the description. If the product has great photos and a compelling description, then most of the time it shows that the seller actually cares about what he or she is doing and will do whatever it takes to keep their customers happy.

Another thing to take care of is shipping.  If the seller offers a shipping method known as e-packet, then the shipping times will be a lot faster than other suppliers. Normally e-packet delivers the product in 2-3 weeks, which is the fastest shipping time you will get on AliExpress, so make sure your supplier provides you with e-packet. Also, to make sure this supplier is reliable, check out how many orders he/she has had; if it is higher than 500 orders, then they are in the clear. If all the points I just described to you check out, then the supplier is a good supplier and you can truly start to grow your business with him or her, and if the supplier doesn't check out on all these points, then find a new one.

One more tip I would share with you, AliExpress tends to take some time when processing a payment. It could take up to three days. It is done simply for their security. If you want to expedite the process of processing the payment for your order to be shipped even faster, then I would recommend using AliPocket. AliPocket is similar to a gift card. It is like a safe credit card for AliExpress, so if you buy AliPocket in bulk and use it to buy the product which you will be shipping out to your client, then there would be no time wasted for processing a payment, and the order will be shipped right away.

Now, AliExpress is great for selling new, trending stuff. But if your goal is to sell fan t-shirts and things of that nature, then it might not be the right choice for you. AliExpress has a lot of things to sell online, but the products it sells are not specific to niches, and people, this is where print on demand t-shirts come in.

What is print on demand, you might ask. Well, print on demand is a service where you come up with a logo, pick out a plain t-shirt, sweater or whatever they have, then what will happen is that the company will use your logo, put it on a t-shirt, etc., and directly ship it out to the customer or the buyer. That is what print on demand is. Now there are a lot of websites to choose from. But the one I highly recommend is Pillow Profits. It is amazing; not only do they have your good old t-shirts, but they also offer things like pillowcases, shower curtains, bed sheets, etc., which can be sent to a customer with your logo on any of those things.

Now print on demand is ideal for those super niche fan pages we talked about before. Since those fan pages are unique and hard to find, you need to be really unique with your products, just like the page you are promoting it to. So, if your store is based on super-niche products, then it would be hard to find products on AliExpress, and this is where print on demand comes in.

What print on demand will offer you is this: cheap supplies with whatever you want on it and fast shipping. Most of the print on demand websites have a really fast delivery since most of them are based in the United States, so you don't need to worry about shipping or any of that. Just make sure to pick out a print on demand website you like and come up with a logo.

Let us talk about building relationships with your suppliers. It is imperative that you build a great relationship with your supplier. Not only will it help you make more profits, but it will also help you get faster shipping times. What I am about to tell you applies more to AliExpress rather than print on demand websites. Regardless of which website it is, you need a great relationship with your supplier, so in order to build great relationships with your suppliers here are the ways you can do so.

Give them business

Be accepting

Leave them great reviews


So, giving them business is quite self-explanatory. If you want to build a great relationship you have to give them business. You can't expect to be their "special customer" if you don't buy anything from them. So make sure you first buy at least 20-25 items before you think about asking them for a discount on your

products. Another thing to be mindful about is making sure you don't get angry at them for a shipment which is a couple of days late, or things of that nature. You have to remember they are trying their best to keep you happy, just like you are trying to keep your customers happy. So make sure you are being accepting and not making a big deal about small things like these. The final thing is to leave a positive review because, let us face it, everyone cares about positive reviews. If you follow all these steps, you will start to build a great relationship with your supplier and you can slowly start to ask for things like discounts on your orders, which would mean a higher profit margin for you. So make sure you start to build a great relationship with them.

With all that said, that is all for finding a supplier for people using online dropshipping. Let's talk about finding suppliers for people using Amazon

FBA or warehouse dropshipping. It is a little bit different but shares some of the same principles.

## Warehouse dropshipping

To find suppliers or products for this type of dropshipping is a little bit easier compared to online dropshipping. Since you can inspect all the product before you start selling, it makes it one step easier compared to the others. So, in short, there are three ways you can go about finding a supplier. The first one is using sites like AliExpress, the second one is to find a warehouse where they are selling the products for cheap, and finally buy products on special sales and re-sell them.

Now, you already know how to find the right supplier on AliExpress, but let's talk about how you can use AliExpress for warehouse dropshipping. So right off the bat, once you find a product that you would like to sell I would highly recommend you buy one of the products and really check its quality. Once you have checked it out and made sure that the quality is of a high caliber, then you should contact the supplier and work out a deal. You see, since you will be buying the product in bulk there would be more chance of you actually getting it for a further discounted price, so make sure you ask for it so you can make even more profit. Finally, once that is all done, ship it to the warehouse and start selling.

That was using AliExpress. Now, let's talk about using warehouse or special sales to find your supplies. People don't realize that there are a lot of warehouses like Costco where you can buy stuff for cheap and sell it on Amazon. So the way this process works is simple. Go to a warehouse like Costco, find a product in bulk for really cheap, and then transport it to Amazon's warehouse and start selling. Trust me, I have found so many cheap products at Costco for sale which have made me some great profits! Make sure you find these products and start selling them on Amazon.

Finally, one of the ways I have made tremendous amounts of money on Amazon FBA is by waiting for sales like Black Friday, and things of that nature. I would buy products on sale for 50% to even 70% off, and after the sale is done I would sell it on Amazon at its original price. Although this method is not as frequently occurring as the other two, it will yield you a lot of profits, so make sure you wait for these sales to make some real cash.

Finally, one secret method I have used before is finding listings on Craigslist and Facebook marketplaces for products and supplies. Most of the time, you will find brand new stuff for sale near you, and the seller would be selling it off for next to nothing. So this would be your time to shine. Find something in bulk for really cheap on these websites, work out a deal, and sell it off on Amazon for a great profit. Now if you find something for cheap but the quantity is low, then I would recommend using eBay to sell it on. I remember finding a brand new iPhone for super cheap, so just like anyone else would do, I bought it and sold it off on eBay for a great profit. So whatever you can find on these websites for cheap, make sure to act on them as soon as possible before they are gone.

So to conclude this chapter, I would just like to remind you how important it is to have the right supplier. A great supplier can either make your business or break it.  Making sure you have the right supplier is imperative, as it will only help you have a longer sustained business. So please, make sure you read this chapter very carefully and practice all the tricks and techniques taught in this chapter in order for you to find the right supplier. Don't settle for a product or supplier which "gets the job done." If you want your business to be the best it can be, then find a product or supplier which would be the best you can find in terms of service quality, and of course the price. But also don't forget to keep your suppliers happy; like I said, if you want better deals on your products you need to make sure your relationship with your supplier is great.

That's all for this chapter; see you on the next one.

# CHAPTER 5: FINDING A HIGHLY PROFITABLE PRODUCT

Does anyone remember the product, the fidget spinner? It came out a couple of years ago and it was really famous. As you can imagine, it made a lot of money, from the people who created it to anyone who sold it. Whoever sold the product when it was at its peak made a whole lot of money. People were buying that product like it was water; it truly became a necessity. It was wild!

You see, the fidget spinner is an example of a highly profitable product, and from the title, you might have guessed it, yes, we are going to be talking about highly profitable products and how to find them. Now here's the good news: finding a profitable product is easy, but to sell it at the right place and the right time is when it gets a tad bit tricky.

Before we get started with this chapter I want to tell you what a product is and the different types of products. So, a product is something you trade or give someone for money.... mostly money. Now there are two types of products. The first one is a commodity product, and the second one would be considered a niche product. A commodity product would be something every human needs for survival. A couple of examples would be bread, water, car, etc. These products are needed by most people so they can survive or sustain a certain lifestyle, which means they will do whatever it takes to get these products to survive.

Now the other product is a niche based product. A niche product would be something people don't buy out of necessity; rather they buy it because they like it. So an example of these products would be dog bracelets, GI Joes, etc. So by no means would you need these products for survival, but there is definitely a need for them.

Ideally, we would all like to sell in the commodity niche as there is a constant demand for it. But to sell things of the commodity type would be a bit challenging, since the people who are at the top of the food chain have spent so much money on the commodity products that in order for you to sell and actually make good money, you would have to spend a lot of money on advertisement. Now, to get into a niche product can work and can make you money. But even though there is less competition, it can be hard to get into.

Remember the fidget spinner I was talking about earlier? What kind of product do you think it is? Commodity or a niche product? If your answer was niche, then you are completely wrong. A fidget spinner was a combination of both commodity AND a niche product. The fidget spinner was a product which was made for people who needed something to fidget with, and through advertising and popularity became a commodity. Do you see where I"m going with this? If you want to find a winning product, find one which is both a commodity product and a niche based product.

So how do you actually go about finding a commodity product and a niche product? Let's discuss. As we know, clothing is worn by everyone and everyone will buy clothes, some people more often than others. If someone is selling a puppy, would you honestly buy it? Would it be a commodity? No, you don't need to have a puppy to survive. It is more of an interest or a niche specific thing to get a puppy. Now for a puppy fan who isn't ready to take on a responsibility of a puppy, what would he or she buy? A puppy or a really cool puppy t-shirt? Obviously a puppy t-shirt. When you combine a commodity product with a niche based product, you really start to create something beautiful. So make sure you create or find something like that.

Now, that is one example of finding or creating a winning product. The next place you can actually find great products to start selling online would be using a website called Thieve.co. This website is impressive; not only does it show the most trending product right now on the market but it also hooks you up with the seller. You know what the best part about this website is? It's that it shows the most trending products based on niche, so if you want to find your winning product to sell online, then I would definitely check out Thieve.co.

Also, if you remember, I spoke about Amazon, to find a niche to sell into. Well, Amazon can be used for finding a winning product as well! If you go into the best sellers rank and look up the top 100 best seller products, then chances are, you will find a product that sells for you. Guys, don't forget, Amazon is the biggest e-commerce store, so if people are actually buying from Amazon, that means it sells. Another website you can use it AliExpress. If you want to find a winning product, then go on AliExpress and look at the best sellers. Since most of the dropshippers use AliExpress as their supplier for their dropshipping business, if the product sells on AliExpress, it most likely will sell for you, because drop-shippers are selling it to their customers. Another great technique is to check out other Shopify websites and to check out what they are selling. Sometimes checking out your competitors' products can help you find that winning product you have been looking for. One of the ways I find out about other Shopify websites is by going to Shopifyexchange.com. What they do is sell Shopify websites which are already making money, so if I were you, I would go on their website and check out their winning products and try and sell them in your store. And most of the time, it works.

The final tool I would recommend is using a software called Dropship Spy. It is a software which shows you the newest and the latest products online, and although there a small amount to be paid for it, it is totally worth it. If you are really serious about starting your dropshipping business, I would recommend you get this software. Just be aware that this system is more for online dropshippers rather than warehouse dropshippers, so keep that in mind.

After you have done everything to find your winning product, what you need to know is how to advertise it. You will not find out how good the product is or how "revolutionary" the product is unless you advertise it and try to sell it. Don't worry, in the next chapter we will talk about how to advertise your product the right way using Facebook and other various tools. If the product doesn't sell after following all the steps above, then find out what you did wrong in finding the right product, then rinse and repeat. Find a new product to sell and make sure you don't make any mistakes this time, finding a new product. You will not find a winning product in your first try, unless you are very fortunate. The point is that it may take time and research to find the right product to sell for your drop shipping, so be patient and stay true to the process, and you will eventually find your winning product.

So that is all the things I wanted to talk about in this chapter. Make sure you follow everything I have said in this chapter if you want to find a winning product. If you have a feeling that this new product you stumbled upon might be the next fidget spinner, then do your research, make sure that you are correct and take the risk. Although it is important to be safe and smart about investing in a new product, sometimes it is also important that you take some risks. Sometimes those risky products yield the best results, which end up making you money. Finally, for people out there trying to create a commodity and niche product in one, make sure whatever you're selling really hits the buyer emotionally. People will buy anything if it attracts them emotionally, so make sure the product isn't more of a commodity product to a niche or vice versa. That is all for this chapter; see you in the next one.

If you're enjoying this book, I would appreciate it if you went to the place of purchase and left a short positive review. Thank you

# CHAPTER 6: HOW TO MARKET YOUR BUSINESS

By now, this book has commented on all major aspects of  dropshipping, from the different types of dropshipping businesses, how to start your own dropshipping business, and how to pick out the most profitable niche and products. You see, everything is important for your business to flourish, but if you can't get people to come onto your page/website or drive traffic to it, then nothing in this book will help you get sales. It's simple;  if no one is there to see your product or what you're selling, then no one is going buy your product.  It's just going to sit there and do nothing. So for you to make sales, you need to drive some traffic to your store or page, and that is what we will be talking about in this chapter:  how to drive traffic to your store or page.

Learning how to drive traffic can be a challenging task.  There is no right or wrong answer in this method. For some people, using websites like Facebook and Instagram could work amazingly and that is all they do to drive traffic, whereas for others, using free traffic techniques could be working beautifully, making them some serious sales. So, it is more trial and error than getting it right in the first place.

When I started my dropshipping business, I tried everything, from Facebook ads to free traffic techniques like creating blogs, and sending out emails. But all my dropshipping businesses work differently, and sometimes one business would work great on getting Facebook traffic and only that, while others might work great on blog traffic or emails, so it really just depends. So to find out what works and what doesn't, you need to try it out and see for yourself. There is no way to tell if a specific ad will generate you millions of dollars or not.

We will talk about the three biggest ways to drive traffic to your product page or website, which are Facebook ads, Instagram shout outs and finally, free traffic utilizing blogs, emails, etc. Try all of them to see which works out best for you. You may find more success with one rather than the other. In my opinion, the hardest one is Facebook. So let's tackle that first.

## Facebook

Facebook has over 2 billion users. So naturally, there will be many people on Facebook who may be interested in buying your products. Facebook advertisements have been used by almost every dropshipper you can find to drive traffic. This method is probably the cheapest and the most effective method you can use to drive traffic to your product page or store. Now, there are some steps you need to go through before you start advertising your product the right way by utilizing Facebook, which we will be going through in this chapter.

First things first. When you create your Facebook ads account, you will need to make sure you add your website pixel on it. This is important for people using the online dropshipping method. Here is the thing; if you don't add your store pixel onto your Facebook ads account, it will not be able to collect data for your website and products. The pixel will collect things like what kind of people are checking out your product page and what kind of people are actually purchasing your product, which would equal a  better ad campaign in the future, as you would be able to target specific people to your product page or website. Now, after you have created your Facebook ads account and added your pixel to your Facebook ads account, we can now start to advertise your products. Here is what we need to take care of before we start advertising on Facebook:

Finding products like yours

Finding big companies' Facebook ads

Targeting to a certain age group and country

Amazing product photos

Amazing captions

Split testing

I know, there are a lot of things to worry about. But believe it or not, these are just the basics we need to take care of, as there a lot of other advertising methods which can be used. But for now, worry about the basics.

So let's start off with the first step. Finding a similar product to yours on Google is important to look for, as most of the time it will show you the top sellers of your niche. When you start your Facebook ad campaign, it will ask you for ad pages or companies related to your niche. Our job is quite simple, yet important. The first thing we will do is go online and search up our product. For example, if I am selling a car, I will look up "cars for sale," then I would click on all the websites which sell our products. So in this hypothetical scenario, I would be clicking through Honda, Toyota, etc. So, after you do that, I want you to write down all the websites which are related to the niche or product that you are going to be selling.

After you have all the top websites, I want you to log into Facebook. Then after that is done, I want you to search up the websites' Facebook pages. Once you have done that, check to see if their Facebook likes are over 500,000, and if so, you have found a winner. You see, what Facebook does with that information on your campaign is this; it will promote your product to the specific people on that page. So let's get back to my hypothetical scenario. If I am selling a car and I add Honda to my targeted Facebook advertisement, it will then specifically target people who are interested in Honda. So find: one, a product, two, a Facebook page which has over 500k followers, and three, the product to the people interested in that page.

Now that you have the keywords and the specific people you will be advertising your products to, it is now time to create an eye-catching advertisement. Since most of you haven't created a Facebook advertisement, I assume, so in order for you to make sure your advertisement converts into sales you will need to make sure your ads look good. Now there are many tips and techniques out there spelled out by "supposed" dropshipping gurus, but some of you might have heard the phrase "If it ain't broke, don't fix it," meaning that if there are big companies advertising their products successfully, then there is no need to come up with your own different unique way of doing it, as that trial and error could hurt your wallet.

If you did your research and tried to find big websites or companies specific to your niche, then there is a high chance that you might have seen their Facebook ads pop up. The next time you see them, I really want you to examine their advertising and see what kind of video or images they are using. This will help you build your own advertisement, so make sure you review the ads and copy what they are doing. Trust me, it will work a lot better than you creating your own special ones.

Let's talk about finding age groups and country for your advertisements. If you know what your product provides to consumers, you would know what kind of people would be interested in purchasing your products. Before you start your first campaign on Facebook, it will ask you to put an age range on your advertisement. So if you are going to be selling a car like I am, then I would probably set the age range around 25 to 65 as most of the people 18 years old won't be buying one by themselves and anyone over 65 won't either. So our goal is to target people who are most likely to buy your product, so this takes some research and there some guesswork involved. But if you really specify the age, you will save a good amount of money and get more sales.

Whereas for picking out the country or region to advertise it to, I would recommend you advertise it to the US only if your budget is small. Most of your buyers will be coming from the United States, so no need to worry about advertising it to any other people. Now, if you have some spare change left over, then you can extend your audience to Canada, which could get you more views and more sales.

After you have done all of this research it's now time to create your advertising image and caption. People don't realize how important it is for you to have the right image and caption for your post. This will either make your post or break it. So picking out the right photo and caption is imperative for your advertisement to be a success. Now how do you pick out the right image for your advertisement? Simple; if you did your research correctly looking up big companies' websites, then you will know the specific type of photo or caption to use, so mimic their advertisement.

Now, after you have decided upon the photos and caption you will be going with, it is now time to add the photo to your campaign. Two things to remember: make sure the photo is high-definition. If it is not high-definition, then it won't stand out from the crowd and it will also look unprofessional. Also make sure the photo is compatible on a smartphone advertisement. To check out what it would look like on a smartphone, simply click on the smartphone advertisement option. It will show you what it looks like.

Now let's talk about the caption. For you to get people clicking on the caption you need to make sure that it is eye-catching. To deliver a great caption you need to make sure you offer your clients some incentives, such as "GET THIS NOW. 50% OFF" or "ONLY 50 LEFT IN STOCK". In the same manner that big firms advertise, you will need to make sure you create urgency by adding an incentive.

Finally, when everything is good to go and ready to be launched, you can utilize a tool called split testing. What you have to do is create two similar advertising campaigns with slight changes. For example, one ad could have an age group of 18-50 and the other 25-65. After the ad has been running for some time, it will show you which one works better compared to the other. This will help you optimize your ad campaigns in the future. This is optional but highly recommended.

That is all for Facebook advertising. Let's now talk about Instagram Influencer advertising.

## Instagram

Instagram is a great place to advertise your products. They have an enormous number of users and most of the time they are more engaged, as compared to Facebook. So if you are thinking about dismissing the idea of advertising on Instagram, think again, as you would be leaving a lot on the table. Note that advertising from Facebook does go on onto Instagram, but it isn't as potent as it should be. So when advertising on Instagram, we use a method called "Instagram Influencer." What it is is quite simple. First, you will find an Instagram page which is related to your topic. Second, you will ask them to promote your product on their Instagram page, and finally, see sales come in. I have used a lot of methods, but this one always works! If you want quick sales on your Instagram account, use this method. Now let's talk about the things you need to worry about before you start advertising on Instagram:

Find the right influencer

Make sure they don't have any bots

Engagement

So, the thing is, for you to make sales and rack up a reasonable amount of cash from your sales, you will need to make sure that your influencer has the right audience. You cannot expect to make sales off of a dog bracelet if the page is about "I hate dogs." This would not make sense. Make sure the product you are trying to sell is related to the audience who relate to that specific page. So for example, if I want to sell a fishing rod, I would look up, say, fishing areas, or great places to fish, and promote there.

Now, before you go out finding your influencer page, you need to make sure that the page has at least 300k followers. If it doesn't, then you are not going to get the engagement you are looking for.

Next thing to take care of would be making sure the influencer you are thinking about working with has a great engagement rate. If people are not tuning into their page ,they probably won't see your ads as well. There are some tools you can use to find that out,  but if someone is not getting at least 5-10% of their  followers, meaning if they have 100k followers and they are not getting at least  5-10k likes, then the chances are, the followers are not engaging.

This would also show you if the followers are bots or not, meaning if they have bought followers or if they are real followers.

Now let's talk about how to get a shout from these Instagram pages.  Message them directly, saying you want a shout out. Then once you guys work out a deal, ask them for a "story shout out," as those work the best.  Ask for a 12-hour story shout

out; all the followers will see your advertisement within the 12 hours, so no need to advertise it longer than you should.

With that being said, let's now discuss the third method.

## Blogs and emails

This method works great! If someone has already bought from you once, and they liked the product or your services, chances are they will buy from you again. Using tools like creating your own blogs or anything of that nature can work beautifully for you to get sales and or to get some traffic into your store, so there are a lot of ways you can get free traffic. We will only be talking about the two main ones today, which would be creating a blog, and collecting an email list. Now there is a downside to this method. It could take some time to get traffic to your blog and collecting an email list, so don't consider this method if you want fast results.

Using blogs and email lists to promote your products and services have been used for some time now, a lot of successful dropshipping businesses solely use this method to advertising their products and services. So it works, and it works great! Just remember, it won't work right away as it takes time.

Now, with that said, here are three things you need to worry about before you start advertising with this method:

Create a blog

Get traffic on the blog

Collect email subscribers

Email them, not SPAM!


So, the first thing you need to do is to create a blog. You will need to create a blog in order for you to actually start collecting emails. So how you actually collect emails is quite simple, Once you have created a blog, I want you to start publishing about the niche or subject which relates to your store or product. For example, if your online store or your product is regarding fishing, then write a blog about "how to ice fish," etc. Make sure the blog you write is filled with knowledge. People would not want to subscribe to a blog if it is not interesting or providing them with great tricks and tips about the niche.

Now, once you have created a blog and written your first blog, you will now need to start promoting your blog to the right people. This can be done for free; all you have to do is go on Google and search up similar blogs posted in the 24 hour mark time. Go on their blog's comment section and tell every reader to check out your link! It works great and equals free traffic.

After you have started to get some traffic onto your website, it will now be time to collect some emails. In order for you to collect emails, offer them something. So, if your blog and store are related to fitness, offer them a free workout plan if they enter their email! Everyone wants free stuff, so make sure you offer it to them. This should help you collect your email list. I have personally built up around 10,000 email lists using this technique, so make sure you use it.

Once you have a good amount of emails you can now start promoting your products. But there is one thing you should not forget: this is not spam! People do not like to see a sales email every day, so make sure you space it out. Ideally here is how you should go about emailing your potential client. For the first four days, send them an educational email like "How to Fish" or "How to Workout," again, something related to your website, and then on the fourth day, you can try and promote your product. This strategy normally works for me, and I am certain that it would work for you.

Now, with that said, I would like to finish off this chapter. Please remember that not all of your advertising or ad campaigns will work. Some might fail and some might work and make you a lot of profit. Your job is to find out what works for you and what doesn't. So trial and error is the answer, but if you follow everything to a T, then you will see success quicker than you had expected. Also, don't forget to try every method out before you knock it, because some methods take time and they might work great for you later on, so keep trying. Success will eventually come your way.

# CONCLUSION

Thank you for sticking it through and reading *Dropshipping: How to generate passive income using e-commerce advanced strategies, Shopify, Amazon FBA and eBay* till the end. I just hope this information was super useful for you to start your very own dropshipping business. The information and knowledge in this book can be useful to a beginner all the way to advanced dropshippers, as the knowledge in this book comes from experience.

The next step for you would be to read all the chapters very carefully, and make sure that whatever is written in the book is absorbed by your brain. From picking out the method you will be using for dropshipping, all the way to finding the right niche to get into reading and finalizing it. Write down notes if you have to, do whatever you can in order to make sure the knowledge in the book doesn't go to waste.

Once you have finally absorbed all the knowledge in this book, I want you to act on it. Act on your goals; if your goal is to start dropshipping to start earning money, then do it! Don't wait. Most people tend to learn about a new topic or business and most of the time they do start, but they give up as soon as they hit their first road bump.

You have to remember that in any business there will be ups and downs so don't expect everything to go smoothly and efficiently. You will fail sometimes. Sometimes you will lose some money. That's the cold hard truth. But if you keep going at your goals, you will eventually get there. Just remember to start and to not give up.

Finally, I would like to remind you this. Every successful person failed at first before he achieved his or her goal. Do you think Jeff Bezos grew his company to where it is today by not facing any adversity? Probably not. Look, I am not trying to scare you before you get into this business. I am just motivating you to not give up as most people do. Just remember that everything takes time and hard work, so keep going at it. If you really want it, it will happen for you. Just work hard and don't give up. Success is on its way!

www.ingramcontent.com/pod-product-compliance
Lightning Source LLC
Chambersburg PA
CBHW030525210326
41597CB00013B/1029